Prince
Charles

The Sustainable Prince

Prince Charles: The Sustainable Prince
© 1997, 1998 by Joan Veon

**THE WOMEN'S INTERNATIONAL
MEDIA GROUP, INC.
P.O. BOX 77
MIDDLETOWN, MD 21769
301/371-0541 www.womensgroup.org**

ISI

Prince Charles

The Sustainable Prince

Joan M. Veon

Businesswoman and Independent Journalist

Dedication

First Printing:
To my brother-in-law, Rodney Pierce,
who went to heaven on September 10, 1997

Second Printing:
To all those who have stood for the Constitution
and Christian principles,
and who have stood in the gap since 1945.
Of those known to me who have stood the longest:

Miss Frances Bacon
Mrs. Gene Birkland
Mrs. Peggy Cuddy
Dr. Dennis Cuddy
Mr. William J. Gill
Mr. Robert Goldsbourgh
Mr. Des Griffin
Mrs. Maureen Heaton
Mrs. Marion Hurley
Mrs. Charlotte Iserbyt
Mrs. Virginia Meves
The Minutewomen
Dr. Stanley Monteith
Mr. Otto Otepka
Col. Archibald Roberts

To those who seek truth
and are not afraid to stand in the gap.
To my husband, Rod Veon,
who is my life partner and supporter.
To my parents, Albert and Mary Yocco.

Table of Contents

Preface

In 1989 or 1990, I prayed a prayer that I had never prayed before. I asked God to reveal truth to me. I prayed not out of fear that I did not know truth, for I assumed that as a Christian I knew the truth automatically. God, so gently, began to show me that I knew nothing of what was really going on in the world, and that much of what I had based my Christianity on was not truth, but the ideas and thoughts of man. I found that what man thinks is based on the media-produced news—news which is not reporting the whole truth about current events on the global level which are setting in place political, spiritual, moral, economic, and social bondage.

In September 1994 I was prompted to go to the United Nations Conference on Population and Development in Cairo, Egypt. At the time I had no knowledge of who the participants were or what they were doing in the world. The only thing I knew about the United Nations was that they were "peacemakers." As a result of my experience in Cairo, my life changed and the focus of what the Lord was showing me changed as He began to reveal truth to me. I was then challenged to attend a number of other conferences in order to "raise the awareness" of what was happening on the global level and how it would affect each one of us. To date, I have attended more than thirty-six United Nations and United Nations-related conferences on four continents. These conferences have dealt with social, environmental, and economic issues as they are part of the greater picture of world government.

The foundational philosophy cementing each of these areas into one is "sustainable development," which is a merger of capitalism and communism. Our form of government is being replaced by a parallel form of government called public-private partnerships, which is a marriage between businesses and government, otherwise known as fascism (see chapter seven).

The implementation of sustainable development, which is taking place on all levels of government, coupled with public–private partnerships, will lead to a complete loss of private property rights and our constitutional freedoms. I have tried to show through the activities of Prince Charles how he is changing the world. Basically, the equation to the global level is this: Sustainable Development (Communism and Capitalism) equals Governance (government) equals Public-Private Partnerships equals ONE (government).

My research has included reading over three thousand pages of United Nations documents and related books and papers, and asking questions of key people in the United Nations and its various commissions and agencies, World Bank officials, past and present world leaders, and high officials in the Clinton administration. In addition, I have had in-depth interviews with numerous people in high places in these same organizations, as well as several interviews with the Prince of Wales Business Leaders Forum. Lastly, I have been an eyewitness to what is transpiring on the global level. My job is to help you understand this complex, deceptive, evil agenda and how it is affecting, and will affect, each one of us. This is needed for the sake of the Kingdom. How are we to stand in the gap if we do not know what is going on around us?

Of those who maintain that world government is part of prophecy, I ask this very simple question: If your house were on fire, would you sit back and watch it burn, knowing insurance statistics say one house in your neighborhood was going to be destroyed, or would you work to hold back and stop the fire? It is time to understand where the fire is so that we can use the greatest weapons we have—knowledge, prayer, and fasting—in order to stand in the gap. We *can* hold back unrighteousness. The time is NOW, but to do so we must know the truth about how the global level is impacting us.

The book you are about to read deals with the business and global pursuits of Prince Charles. Interestingly enough, these are not part of the daily reports that we receive on radio and television. As a result of the tragic death of Diana, Princess of Wales, on August 31, 1997, you will find a eulogy to her memory. It was Dr. Noah Hutchings who suggested this be added. While I do not want to take away from what you are about to read, Diana's life and death do make a statement about the prince, the man whom the press has shown us is not the real Charles. Diana knew the real Charles. In her last interview with the BBC's "Panorama," she talked about the fact that her popularity was something he could not handle, as he had been accustomed to all of the attention. She pointed out that her popularity caused a rift in their marriage, which was in addition to the "other woman." Diana said, "I was a problem, I was a liability. This had not happened before."

As we go into the fourth printing, other than several new appendices to make additional comments, there is not much more to add. This book is complete and timeless in its documentation of the major religious, political, philosophical, and corporate changes which the world is undergoing and the man responsible for making them.

—Joan Veon
Olney, Maryland, July 25, 2000

Diana,
The Unfulfilled Princess

I remember sixteen years ago watching with happiness the "fairy tale" wedding of Prince Charles to Lady Diana Spencer. Over the years, "shy Di," as she was called, became the heroine of the common person. Her growth in grace and stature was not without a lot of bumps, mistakes, and heartache. Life was difficult for her, however, and at times the inward turmoil was reflected on her face and body. Because of the people's love for her, Diana acquired the poise and confidence needed as they affirmed her sense of worth throughout her marriage to the Prince of Wales.

A lonely child, Diana was a product of divorce, and divorce was the last thing she wanted for herself and her children. I am sure when she married the prince she believed in her own fairy tale. Unfortunately, this is not how her life turned out. She remarked in a very candid, spontaneous interview with "Panorama," "There were three of us in the marriage. It was a bit crowded." As a result of the unconventional ways she chose to get attention, such as the book by Andrew Morton exposing the true situation, Diana went against the grain of the British royal family, ostracizing herself even further.

More telling than anything else about life in the palace was a short phrase from that same "Panorama" interview overlooked by most people. She said the reason for the surprise interview was that "they wanted to put me away."

In June 1997 Princess Diana came to Washington, D.C., to give a press conference at the American Red Cross on land mines. I was there as press. My purpose was different from that of the other journalists, as I had observed the deep loneliness and lack of meaning in her life as she used her beauty to gain any kind of attention she could get. In Diana's search to assuage her deep need for the love her husband was giving to someone else, she took lovers whom she hoped would love her for herself.

For a number of years I had prayed for her salvation. In June 1996 when I went to the United Nations Conference on Human Settlements in Istanbul, Turkey, my roommate was an English-woman who had a great love and concern for Diana. One morning we both prayed with great intercession that she would come to know Jesus Christ as her Lord and Savior. As her separation from Prince Charles became final in the form of a divorce, I continued to pray for her.

I was ecstatic when I heard she was coming to Washington, D.C. I immediately called the American Red Cross to see how I could attend the press briefing. My desire was to bring her a gift—a Bible. I did that, purchasing for her a small, red, leather-bound King James Bible. I attached a little card which said I had been praying for her and wanted her to know that the only place she would find peace was in a personal relationship with Jesus Christ. I wrote, "Peace is not to be found in fame, fortune, power, sex, or money, but with the Son of God." At the Red Cross, I mentioned to several people that I had a gift for Diana and their excitement showed. I was directed to a gentleman who told me he would give it to her and he asked for my card. I told him that I was giving her my favorite book!

As we were waiting for Diana to come out for the press briefing, a lady who had just taken a seat on the marble structure near where I was standing struck up a conversation with me. I asked her where she was from and she told me the BBC—she and her crew had just flown in for this press briefing. She said she could not imagine why the news desk wanted more coverage when Diana had given a similar press briefing the previous week in London. I told her that I had a lot of admiration for the princess. When she asked why, I explained that I saw Diana as a survivor, reminding her of the spontaneous "Panorama" interview in which Diana defended herself against the royal family who, she said, had wanted to put her away. The journalist recalled the interview, but had not thought of it the way I did. I told her anyone who would tell the queen of England that she did not want her son, was a survivor. She asked me when Diana had done that and I responded, "When she told Charles that she would not stay in a crowded marriage." Interestingly, the lady from the BBC found what I had to say revealing as she had not considered the information in the same way as I had.

As a result of standing near the BBC while they were doing an on-site news report, Diana looked over to see what they were doing. I was able to look straight at her, and she at me. I have no doubt that our eyes met as I prayed over her that day, asking God to help her recognize her need for Jesus.

There are many, many Dianas in this world. The difference between Diana, the Princess of Wales, and those who are unknown is that the princess had everything—position, fame, fortune, power, and love from people all over the world. However, she did not have Jesus Christ, who is the Way, the Truth, and the Life. No man or woman comes to God except those who first find Jesus Christ as Lord and Savior. That is our mission, that is our purpose, there is no other. It is Jesus, Jesus, Jesus.

Whether or not the Red Cross official gave my gift to Diana, I do not know. But this I know—I did what I was asked to do and what was needed. Blessed be the name of the Lord.

Conclusion

The British royal family is "royal." They are excessively rich, and they hold great position not only in Britain but worldwide. They are addressed as "Her or His Royal Highness," have people curtsy or bow when being presented, have people walk behind them if they are of a lesser birth or rank, and wear gloves when meeting commoners (the Queen, Queen Mother, Princesses Anne and Margaret). The countries of the world are visited by the royal family on a regular basis.

Just *who* are these people? Where *do* they get their authority? What *does* it really mean? Are we the prize? Just who *is* Prince Charles? What *is* his real objective?

And the ten horns which thou sawest are ten kings, which have received no kingdom as yet; but receive power as kings one hour with the beast. These have one mind, and shall give their power and strength unto the beast. These shall make war with the Lamb, and the Lamb shall overcome them: for he is Lord of lords, and King of kings: and they that are with him are called, and chosen, and faithful.

—Rev. 17:12–14

Introduction

There are many who believe we are in "the last days," an opinion based on the regathering of the nation of Israel in 1948. As such, there has been great speculation as to who might be part of the end-time cast of players. The following is written to bring to your awareness a man who has been a major "mover and shaker" behind the world scenes and who is now becoming more public as a result of his global projects. Because of his seemingly passive understanding of life, he has been considered "daft" or incapable of anything of great importance. His title and lineage alone are reasons to keep your eyes on him. However, his whole being, his logos—what he is, what he does, what he believes, and what he says—beg a deeper look at Prince Charles, heir to the oldest and most powerful throne in the world.

However, our look cannot only deal with the man, but must deal with his politics which demand both an empowered United Nations and empowered multinational corporations. The politics of the prince, specifically his environmental philosophy, are enshrouded in "sustainable development," which is a merger between communism and capitalism. This merger, then, necessitates a new form of governance through public-private partnerships (fascism). The picture is complete when one considers both the empowered United Nations (which the royal family directs) and the empowered multinational corporations (which Charles influences through the Prince of Wales Business Leaders Forum). When all of these are placed into operation through public–private partnerships, all of society as we know it will change. We must understand each of these things in order to know the "day and hour."

The incredible fascination I have with British royalty, and specifically Prince Charles, began when I applied for my first library card at twelve years of age. Not knowing where to begin reading, I asked the librarian to help me. That kind lady instructed me to follow as she went to a corner of the huge room. Pulling a book off a shelf the librarian said, "You can begin with this one and when you are finished, you can read the rest of the books on this shelf, and then those on the shelf beneath it." While I do not remember the exact name, it was on the early life of Queen Elizabeth I, "Good Queen Bess." I did exactly what the librarian suggested and read the rest of the books on that shelf about Queen Elizabeth I. The other shelf contained books on Queens Victoria and Elizabeth II and a number of other British royal family members.

Over thirty years later I attended my first United Nations (UN) conference in Cairo, Egypt. Although I had written an economic newsletter for a number of years, I was not familiar with the United Nations, the World Bank (WB), the International Monetary Fund (IMF), or any other global agency. While researching and writing my newsletter in 1992, I became convinced that the fall of the dollar against the German deutsche mark and Japanese yen was part of a concerted move toward a "world currency." However, a world or global currency would not be necessary unless there were a world government . . . but who? It was not until I went to Cairo that I understood through my conference experience that the United Nations *is* world government. This conclusion was very obvious throughout the conference proceedings, as was the blatant orchestration by the United Nations and the U.S. State Department to achieve some type of consensus for the radical global agenda being pushed on the people of the world.

My Cairo "experience" led to more conferences and a great deal of reading of United Nations documents. While it was very obvious the United Nations has tremendous power, after a while it became even more obvious that there must be additional powers behind the UN. The question was, "Who?"

At the June 1995 UN fiftieth anniversary celebrations in San Francisco, I thought it very odd that Britain's Princess Margaret was there. While the princess attended a number of functions, I photographed her at the interfaith service in Grace Cathedral and at the charter ceremony which featured all of the ambassadors to the United Nations, as well as President Clinton. No reason was given for her attendance, and it was *not* reported in any of the major newspapers other than the *San Francisco Examiner*. Also, according to the list of royal engagements as found in *Majesty,* a British magazine that tracks the royal family, her calendar stopped a week before she went to California. *Royalty* magazine (vol. 14, no. 1) then published a picture of Westminster Hall with the caption: "The Queen, accompanied by the Duke of Edinburgh and Prince Charles, joined international delegates at Westminster Hall to mark the 50th anniversary of the United Nations." This coincided with the fiftieth anniversary of the charter ceremony in San Francisco. Both were held on June 26.

In a speech given in London that day, now former Prime Minister John Major spoke of the early beginnings of the United Nations. He said, "At a meeting in London, they developed the idea of 'willing cooperation between free peoples in a world relieved of the menace of aggression.' A blueprint called 'The United Nations Plan for Organised Peace' was drawn up by a [British] foreign office team." He also pointed out that Prince Charles' grandfather, King George VI, was the first head of state to visit the General Assembly.[1] It appears all roads lead to England.

Chapter One

The Rhodes Legacy

Cecil Rhodes

It was Cecil Rhodes, *"the Founder*—of the international diamond industry, of Rhodesia . . . *the Premier*—of the Cape; *the Lawgiver*—of the Glen Gray Act of Rhodesia; *the World Statesman*—confidant of Queen Victoria and Kaiser Wilhelm,"[2] who endowed and set up the Rhodes Scholarship in his seventh will for the purpose of uniting the United States with Great Britain. Rhodes felt there were "too few Britons" as

> too little of the globe was British territory. . . . "If we had retained America there would . . . be millions more of English living. [W]e are the finest race in the world and the more of the world we inhabit the better it is for the human race. Wars would end, too."[3]

He further elaborated:

> The United States was to be recovered and made an "integral part" of the Empire. A system of colonial representation in the British Parliament was to be inaugurated which would "weld together the disjointed members of the Empire" and thus create a power so great that wars would be rendered impossible.[4]

For the record, Cecil Rhodes was both a homosexual and a Mason. It was the last of his seven wills that set up the Rhodes Scholarship program, while the former wills provided parameters for the trustees who were to bring the world back under British rule. Rhodes called his creed a "confession of faith" (please see Appendix G), and said it would be carried out through a secret society. In addition to the Rhodes Trust, other monies used to accomplish his goal include "the Astor fortune [and] certain powerful British banks (of which the chief was Lazard Brothers and company)."[5]

Dr. Carroll Quigley, Bill Clinton's mentor at Georgetown and the man who wrote a letter on Clinton's behalf for the Rhodes Scholarship, wrote two books that are considered epics in understanding the truth about modern history: *Tragedy and Hope* and *The Anglo-American Establishment*. In his second book he wrote that the secret society that would be formed by his Rhodes's will "was to devote itself to the preservation and expansion of the British Empire [which] has been known at various times as Milner's Kindergarten, as the Round Table Group, as the Rhodes crowd, as the *Times* crowd, as the All Souls group, and as the Cliveden set."[6] Lord Milner was the chief trustee after 1901. According to Quigley, "The original members of the Milner Group came from well-to-do, upper-class, frequently titled families."[7] Furthermore, Rhodes outlined men who might be useful members of the secret society. "Men of ability and enthusiasm who find no suitable way to serve their country under the current political system." He (Rhodes) wrote that, "This is to be a kind of religious brotherhood like the Jesuits, 'a church for the extension of the British Empire.'"[8]

In looking to determine how to bring the world under British rule, this secret society, according to Quigley,

> caused the Boer War of 1899–1902; it set up and controls the Rhodes Trust; it created the Union of South Africa in 1906–1910; has been the most powerful single influence in All Souls,

Balliol, and New Colleges at Oxford for more than a generation; it has controlled the *Times* for more than fifty years with
the exception of the three years 1919–1922; it publicized the
idea of and the name "British Commonwealth of Nations" in
the period 1908–1918; it was the chief influence in Lloyd
George's war administration in 1917–1919 and dominated the
British delegation to the Peace Conference of 1919; it had a
great deal to do with the formation and management of the
League of Nations and of the system of mandates; it founded
the Royal Institute of International Affairs in 1919 and still
controls it; it was one of the chief influences on British policy
toward Ireland, Palestine, and India in the period of 1917–1945;
it was a very important influence on the policy of appeasement
of Germany during the years 1920–1940; and it controlled and
still controls, to a very considerable extent, the sources and the
writing of the history of British Imperial and foreign policy
since the Boer War.[9]

Of particular interest with regard to the Milner (Kindergarten)
Group was how the world would be ruled once under the British
Empire. According to Quigley:

> They feared the British Empire might fall into the same diffi-
> culty and destroy British idealism and British liberties by the
> tyranny necessary to hold on to a reluctant Empire. And any
> effort to hold an empire by tyranny they regarded as doomed
> to failure. . . . The Group feared that all culture and civilization
> would go down to destruction because of our inability to con-
> struct some kind of political unit larger than the national state,
> just as Greek Culture and civilization in the fourth century B.C.
> went down to destruction because of the Greeks' inability to
> construct some kind of political unit larger than the city-state.
> This was the fear that had animated Rhodes, and it was the
> same fear that was driving the Milner Group to transform the

British Empire into a Commonwealth of Nations and then place that system within a League of Nations.[10]

The United Nations became the successor to the League of Nations in 1945. While there are a number of major differences between the two organizations, the biggest difference was an empowered United Nations. The decisions of the League [of Nations] Council were essentially recommendations whereas "the decisions of the [United Nations] Security Council are legally binding upon the Members of the United Nations."[11]

It should be noted that the American counterpart to the Royal Institute of International Affairs (RIIA) is the Council on Foreign Relations (CFR), which was founded by David Rockefeller and is still controlled by him. American benefactors to the RIIA include J. D. Rockefeller, Ford Motor Company, and Carnegie trustees. Interestingly, many of the CEOs from American multinational corporations who are partners with the Prince of Wales Business Leaders Forum (discussed fully in chapter eight) are members of the Council on Foreign Relations, the Trilateral Commission, or both. In addition, there is an interconnectedness between U.S. corporations, as many chief executive officers serve as directors on each other's board of directors. This kind of close relationship also exists on the global level where many corporations work with a number of international organizations such as the International Chamber of Commerce (ICC), the World Business Council for Sustainable Development (WBSCD), the World Business Academy, and the International Institute for Sustainable Development (IISD). The Prince of Wales Business Leaders Forum partners with many of these organizations as well.

American Rhodes Scholars

The success of Cecil Rhodes is seen in the change of world view espoused by American Rhodes Scholars. Upon graduation, they come back to the United States to fill prestigious positions in every field of endeavor imaginable. Not one industry or field of study has gone untouched by their Anglo-American views. Rhodes Scholar Basil Blackwell wrote, "As of 1955, there were 17 colleges and universities in which their presidents were Rhodes Scholars,"[12] which included Union Theological Seminary, Atlantic Christian College, Oberlin College, Columbia Theological Seminary, Purdue, the University of Maryland, and Swarthmore, to name a few.

Some of the more recognizable Rhodes Scholars are: President Bill Clinton; Senators (former) Bill Bradley (NJ), Richard Lugar (IN), Paul Sarbanes (MD), Russell Finegold (WI), Larry Pressler (SD), and (former) David Boren (OK); Supreme Court Justice David Souter; (former) Secretary of Labor Robert Reich; (former) Secretary of State Dean Rusk; Baltimore mayor Kurt Schmoke; Library of Congress James Billington; singer and actor Kris Kristofferson, who played in the controversial movie *Amerika;* Edwin Hubbel, for whom the spacecraft is named; and Sir John Templeton, orginator of the Templeton Award for Progress in Religion. In Clinton's first term, he chose twenty-two Rhodes Scholars to serve in key positions.

It should be noted that there are a number of other Anglo-American education programs patterned after the Rhodes Scholarship. They are: the scholarship funded by the John Motley Morehead Foundation at the University of North Carolina;[13] the Fulbright Scholarship established by a bill introduced by Senator Fulbright in 1948; the Marshall Scholarship Schemes; the Davidson Fellowships; the Choate Fellowship to Harvard Law School; the Procter Fellowships at Princeton; the Riggs Fellowship at the University of Michigan; and the Henry Fellowships at Harvard and Yale.[14]

In 1997 Prince Philip came to Washington, D.C., to attend the fiftieth anniversary of the Marshall Plan, for whom the scholarship is named. It was George C. Marshall who delivered an address at Harvard University in 1947 which launched the plan by his name to rebuild Europe. The prince remarked that of the $13 billion in economic aid which was given to Western Europe after World War II, $3 billion went to Great Britain, the single largest beneficiary. Prince Philip explained that

> Parliament passed an Act setting up the Marshall Scholarships Scheme. It pays for 40 brilliant young Americans each year to study for two or three years at a British University. Over the years we have picked well: Marshall Scholars have risen to the top of all three branches of the United States Government: Justice Breyer [appointed by Clinton] and Congressman Spratt; and Interior Secretary Babbitt all studied in Britain under our Marshall programme.[15]

Rhodes had predicted the time when wars would end. "Rhodes 'universal peace' would begin, according to him, 'after 100 years.'" It was "in the autumn of 1990 that President George Bush . . . spell[ed] out his 'new world order' concept for universal peace and cooperation."[16] On March 6, 1991, President Bush spoke of the new world order as "a world in which the United Nations is poised to fulfill the historic vision of its founders."[17] You will recall that before we could attack Iraq, President Bush had to get the approval of the United Nations Security Council. President Clinton, in my opinion, has picked up the new world order mantle by giving the United Nations more recognition and dominance than any other president. Evidence of this is seen in his speeches, the globalist agenda being espoused in every area of government, and the financial support provided to the United Nations through various U.S. departments (state, agriculture, energy, labor, etc.).

The Royal Connection
Up until its fiftieth anniversary, I had not seen any British "royalty" connection with the UN, the successor to the League of

Nations. Although I had found a speech given by Prince Charles in 1992 commending the Brundtland Commission for their work in bringing the term "sustainable development" (discussed later) into everyone's vocabulary,[18] there appeared to be no direct connection until I attended the fifty-first meeting of the IMF/World Bank in October 1996. It was there I happened upon a booklet directly connecting the Prince of Wales with the UN and World Bank. The booklet, published by the Prince of Wales Business Leaders Forum, is entitled *Business as Partners in Development: Creating Wealth for Countries, Companies and Communities,* and is in collaboration with the World Bank and the United Nations Development Programme. What the book revealed is that the prince is a very major player on the global scene—more so than we realize. The question to be asked and answered is: "Who is Prince Charles?"

Chapter Two

The Development of Prince Charles

Prince Charles

Interestingly, Prince Charles was born Charles Philip Arthur George Mountbatten-Windsor in 1948, the same year that Israel was birthed by the United Nations. In 1969 his mother made him Prince of Wales in a ceremony at Caernarvon Castle in Wales. His investiture marked the start of his royal duties as he became a Knight of the Garter. It is members of the Order of the Garter that comprise the Queen's "inner circle" of confidants. According to his biographer, Anthony Holden, "At the same moment [Prince Charles was being invested], across the world, three men were preparing to land on the moon."[19] As the twenty-first Prince of Wales, the future Charles III has an abundance of titles which include: Earl of Chester, Duke of Cornwall, Duke of Rothesay, Earl of Carrick, Baron Renfrew, Lord of the Isles and Great Steward of Scotland, Knight of the Most Noble Order of the Garter, Knight of the Most Ancient and Most Noble Order of the Thistle, and Great Master and Principal Knight Grand Cross of the Most Honourable Order of the Bath. It is the Order of the Bath into which Presidents Ronald Reagan and George Bush were knighted after each left office.

Prince Charles' Lineage

Prince Charles is literally related to everyone of royal blood in

Business as Partners in Development

Creating wealth for countries, companies and communities

Jane Nelson

The Prince of Wales Business Leaders Forum

in collaboration with

The World Bank

and

The United Nations Development Programme

the world, along with a few who are not, like Charles Darwin. According to the English genealogist Gerald Paget, who spent most of his ninety-two years tracing the lineage of Queen Elizabeth and Prince Charles, "HRH's [Prince Charles] breeding is the most important in the world. . . . He is heir to the world's greatest position that is determined solely by heredity."[20] In the introduction to Paget's monumental work, *The Lineage and Ancestry of H.R.H. Prince Charles, Prince of Wales,* Paget writes:

His Royal Highness is cousin or nephew, in varying degrees, of all the six wives of King Henry VIII. He has many descents from the royal houses of Scotland, France, Germany, Austria, Denmark, Sweden and Norway, Spain, Portugal, Russia, and the Netherlands. . . . In addition to Charlemagne and William the Conqueror, he numbers amongst his ancestors such historic characters as King Alfred the Great, King Harold, who was slain at Hastings, Llewelyn the Great Prince of North Wales, Owain Glyndwr, Warwick the Kingmaker, Margaret, Countess of Salisbury (the last of the Plantagenets), the Protector Edward Seymour, the Duke of Somerset and his rival John Dudley, Duke of Northumberland . . . Louis IX, King of France, the Emperor Rudolph of Hapsburg, Catherine I, Empress of Russia, Robert Bruce, Mary Queen of Scots. . . . [21]

Paget notes:

Links through marriages or a common ancestor can be found to such diverse people as Genghis Khan and twelve Presidents of the United States of America (for the last see Burke's *Presidential Families of the United States of America*).[22]

Prince Charles's biographer, Anthony Holden, goes further and explains that the prince descends over and over again from Charlemagne and Frederick Barbarossa and all the great dynasties, Hapsburg and Hohenstaufen, Guelph and Hohenzollern, Bavaria and Saxony, Hesse and Baden. . . . In Italy, his forefathers include the Dukes of Savoy and the Emperor Frederick II . . . and the medieval Kings of Sicily, as also the Orsini of Rome (Pope Nicholas III was his ancestral uncle). . . . In Spain, they include Ferdinand and Isabella . . . and thus El Cid himself. The Prince's Anglo-Saxon and Danish royal forefathers sprang from Dark Age kings who incarnated the storm-spirit Woden (after whom Wednesday is named), and among his pagan Celtic royal forefathers were King Niall of the Nine Hostages and the dynamic Iron Age scral kings of Tara, the great sanctuary of ancient Ireland. Through the Lusignan crusader kings of Cyprus, titular kings of Jerusalem, Prince Charles descends a millennium further back from King Tiridates the Great, the first Christian monarch of all (under whom Armenia was converted in A.D. 314, before even Rome itself), and thus from the divine Parthian imperial House of Arsaces (247 B.C.), which reigned over Persia and Babylonia and was in its time the mightiest dynasty in the Ancient World.[23]

I have it on good authority that Prince Charles is Jewish through his father's father, who was a German Jewish banker. If you compare Charles's lineage to the kingdoms and beasts in Daniel 2 and 7, he descends from those mentioned.

The Rise of Prince Charles

Charles is a complex man with many sides. He is a man of action, having served in the Royal Navy in a number of junior and senior command positions. He is a helicopter pilot and has logged over nine hundred hours flying a wide variety of jet fighter planes, including the Chipmunk, Spitfire, Nimrod, Phantom, Jet Provost, and Harrier T4, to name a few.[24] He enjoys polo and is an

The queen places the coronet on the head of her 19 $\frac{1}{2}$ year-old son, the 21st Prince of Wales.

expert skier. He is an artist and a musician as well as a business-man, maintaining a business that exports organic products throughout Europe and England, in addition to caring for his inherited lands. Charles is a twenty-first century Renaissance man—a man for all seasons. There is one other title he could be given besides the one I have given him and that is, "Philosopher-King."

Unlike his uncle, the Duke of Windsor, who never worked after he stepped down from the throne in 1936, Prince Charles oversees a number of trusts, is involved in organic farming and homeopathic medicine, has been critical of and active in the field of architecture, creating an Institute of Architecture to teach classical thinking and methods to its students in an effort to revive classical architecture, has worked behind the scenes pushing the radical environmental agenda of the United Nations into the forefront of world politics, and if not *the* key, is now one of the leading figures on the face of the globe creating "public-private" partnerships in developing countries. The public-private partnership is the new form of governance (a polite term for government) worldwide. His nonprofit organization, the Prince of Wales Business Leaders Forum (PWBLF), is spearheading this governmental change along with major multinational corporations, most of which have more money than many third world countries.

In a speech at the 1988 European Environment Conference, the prince said:

> There is a growing realisation that we are not separate from Nature; a subconscious feeling that we need to restore a feeling of harmony with Nature and a proper sense of respect and awe for the great mystery of the natural order of the Universe. . . . We are beginning to realise that whatever we do to Nature —whether it is on the grandest scale or just in our own gardens—is ultimately something that we are doing to our own deepest selves.[25]

In order to understand what he is doing, we must discern the personal beliefs that guide him.

Religion and the Prince of Wales

Not happy with the Christian faith, Charles began to search for the meaning of life in the late sixties at Cambridge. According to his biographer, "he began a tentative inquiry into the field of what its practitioners referred to as 'psychical research' or 'parapsychology'—and which its adversaries ridiculed as 'dabbling in the occult.'"[26] In the mid-seventies, South African-born writer, explorer, and mystic Laurens van der Post (who was also a friend of the Queen Mother) became a spiritual counselor to Charles. It was van der Post who helped him explore the natural world as well as the inner world, where "the outer depends on the inner."[27] He went on to study Buddhism and Hinduism, mixing the relationship of the individual to the environment in economic, social, and spiritual terms. The convictions that Charles began to form—"what he was soon to say about alternative medicine, architecture, and the environment, sprang from a spiritual feeling for the mystical in mankind."[28]

The Gaia Hypothesis

Charles was greatly influenced by James Lovelock, a British scientist, who formulated the Gaia hypothesis, which today is known as the worship of the earth, a belief based on the Greek goddess Gaia, the Earth Mother. The concept of "holism," they say, which is a part of Gaia, is based on the principles of harmony, balance, and the interconnectedness of nature with a search for inner awareness. Another way to understand holism is to realize that it perverts and inverts Genesis 1 where man has dominance over the earth, to one in which he is equal with the earth, the plants, and the animals. In the seventies, as a result of his newfound holistic philosophy (radical environmentalism), the prince started to involve himself with organic farming, architecture, and homeopathic medicine. When one analyzes what holism is, considering their definition of man, it means man evolves. Holism is evolution at its finest.

Known as the "green prince" or "eco-prince," Charles, like most radical environmentalists, elevates the position of the environment to one of dominance over man, an inversion of Genesis

1. From his first speech on the environment given at the Countryside Conference in 1970, to his global push for sustainable development and public-private partnerships, Charles maintains that the environment is *key to* changing society—how we live, where we live, and our values. However, any religion that inverts Genesis 1 is paganism, which the apostle Paul wrote about in Romans.

Charles, the Environmental Businessman

When Charles attended Trinity College in the late 1960s, he studied archaeology, anthropology, and history, all of which are key with regard to the environment and architecture. In 1981 he and a "somewhat maverick group of businessmen"[29] formed Business in Community, which today is the Prince of Wales Business Leaders Forum. Business in Community came out of a 1980 Anglo-American Conference on Community Involvement where British tycoons learned of America's success in cleaning up its cities through public-private partnerships, in which the local community joined with businesses and local government in order to afford the changes necessary to revitalize major cities. Public–private partnerships were first developed and used in the 1940s and 1950s when the city of Pittsburgh joined forces with Richard King Mellon and other businessmen to revitalize Pittsburgh.[30] Years later, in March 1988, Charles attended the Remaking the Cities Conference in Pittsburgh where he delivered the keynote address. The Remaking the Cities Conference was a "first in history," as it was a joint partnership between the American and British Institutes of Architecture. According to conference chairman David Lewis, it was Prince Charles who, when he visited the American Institute of Architects in Washington, D.C., initiated the idea of an international forum on urban regeneration to be held in Pittsburgh. The conference had five workshops, one of which was specifically on "creating new partnerships for development." Whether the residents of Pittsburgh, or conference participants, knew it or not, they were discussing the same United Nations environmental concepts and agenda that was later unveiled at the Rio Earth Summit in 1992, and reinforced at the Habitat II Conference in 1996.

By way of human interest, I interviewed one businessman from Pittsburgh who had close and continuous contact with Prince Charles while he was in Pittsburgh. He mentioned that he rode in the prince's Rolls Royce while he showed the prince the city. When I asked if the prince brought his Rolls Royce with him, he replied that he was told by the State Department that the royal family has a Rolls Royce that is kept permanently in Washington. I had the impression that it was kept by the State Department and not the British Embassy because I clarified that point. Prince Charles is protected not by the Secret Service, but by the Department of State when he visits. This man said the prince was very well informed and excited about the future of cities and towns, stating the citizens should envision what they want in their town. The city where I grew up, Racine, Wisconsin, has just been named a "sustainable city" as a result of Sam Johnson, a businessman who serves on the President's Commission on Sustainable Development. Many residents have absolutely *no idea* what sustainable development *really* means, or how the public-private partnerships suggested will shift decision-making and control to a new form of governance.

Note: Governance is their term for government.

Chapter Three

Philosophical Components
of the Agenda

Public-Private Partnerships = Fascism

Interestingly, it was in the early 1970s that the United Nations adopted the environment as its "mantra." Think of all the implications. All of us share the environment; it is a common denominator no matter where you live. The only way to change the laws of every country, and to take control, is to make the environment the focal point. Today, it is the goal of the United Nations to pass laws on the global level that will then be ratified by all of the member states. These laws will impact every country and every citizen, and eventually the world will be ruled by "global governance," which is only possible through public-private partnerships. The key to governance in the twenty-first century is the partnership between business, the private sector, and government, which is fascism.

What is "public-private partnership"? Public-private partnership is just what it says it is. First, it is a business arrangement, sealed by an agreement or, in some cases, a handshake. The terms of the partnership will vary according to partners and objectives. Second, the parties in the partnership are public and private entities. Public entities refer to government—local, county, state, federal, and/or global agencies. Private refers to nongovernmental groups such as foundations, nonprofit groups, corporations, and individuals. For example, foundations could include the Ford, Rockefeller, or the local "good-works" foundation; nonprofits could refer to nongovernmental organizations like the Prince of Wales Business Leaders Forum, the Nature Conservancy, the Sierra Club, World Wildlife Federation, Planned Parenthood, or NOW; and corporations could be any corporation from a small one to a multinational like Exxon, Johnson Wax, 3M, Black and Decker, or Giant Foods. Lastly, individuals could be any person—such as a businessman, rancher, or dentist.

A public-private partnership will always have as its goal a business-making venture that requires some form of "governance." The question is, since the players will vary in experience and wealth, who has the most power? We know from life itself that whoever has the most money has the power. For example, when a public-private partnership is comprised of governments such as the County Department of Environmental Initiatives, the State Department of Environmental Resources; a number of private entities like a land trust (foundation) and the Nature Conservancy (nonprofit); along with a corporation such as Black and Decker, the players with the most money control the partnership. In this case, it would be the Nature Conservancy with assets of over $1 billion, and Black and Decker Corporation with a capitalization of $1.6 billion. Representative government loses.

Public-private partnerships were "unveiled" in June 1996 at the United Nations Conference on Human Settlements, Habitat II, held in Istanbul. It took me nine months of research from the Habitat II Conference to understand what a public-private partnership was. The document which finally helped me to understand its importance and implications was from the *U.S. Man and Biosphere Bulletin* which said:

"The long term goals of the U.S. MAB Program is to contribute to achieving a sustainable society early in the twenty-first century. The MAB mission and long term goal will be implement-

As the Constitution is eroded:

Constitution

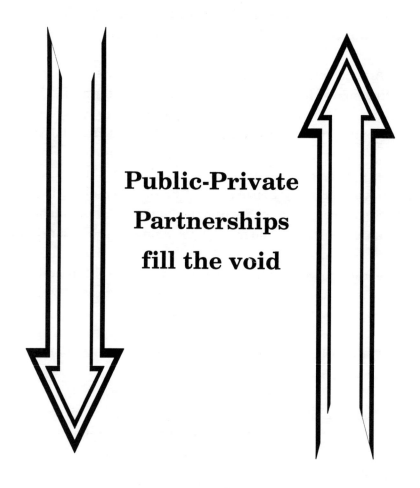

Public-Private
Partnerships
fill the void

Public-Private
Partnerships = Fascism

ed, in the United States and internationally, through public-private partnerships and linkages that sponsor and promote cooperative, interdisciplinary research, experimentation, education, and information exchange on options by which societies can achieve sustainability." Adopted by the U.S. National committee for the Man and Biosphere Program, July 26, 1995.[31]

In an interview I conducted in March 1997 at the Rio+5 Conference with Dr. Wally N'Dow, secretary-general of the Habitat II Conference, he said, "We have got to a point where we cannot not partner with the private sector, as governments, as the civil society, as NGOs, but also as people active in international development such as the United Nations. That is what Istanbul tried to convey."

In a follow-up interview with Dr. Noel Brown, former director of the United Nations Environment Programme and current special advisor to the Group of 77, he said of public-private partnerships:

I believe that the future of the U.N. will rest on effective partnering with the private sector—with business and industry. But I also believe that the environment and the environmental community must also rethink its mission and redefine its role as we enter the phase of globalization and as we are on the threshold of the twenty-first century.

In addition to revitalizing Pittsburgh, public-private partnerships have been used for the last twenty years in America as a method of providing financing to low-income families. HUD and its Office of Community Planning and Development has used public-private partnerships to create affordable housing since 1990. In addition, Maryland, Oregon, and Minnesota have implemented state-level public-private partnerships. It should be noted that as public-private partnerships continue to rise in the U.S., our

Constitution and private property rights are being eroded.

The Club of Rome

There are several books that influenced Charles and helped to form his world view. One is the 1972 Club of Rome report called *The Limits to Growth* which, because of its importance, is highlighted here, and the other is *Small Is Beautiful* by E. F. Schumacher. The Club of Rome started when Dr. Aurelio Peccei, an Italian industrial manager, economist, and visionary, brought thirty people together from ten countries to discuss the present and future predicament of man. From this initial meeting came the organization now called the Club of Rome, which has been described as an "invisible college."[32] The experts who came together did not represent government or the United Nations, we are told, but were from the fields of pollution, agriculture, resources, population, socio-political trends, and capital, to name a few. The Volkswagen Foundation funded their project. (It should be noted that Volkswagen is one of the advisory members of the Prince of Wales Business Leaders Forum.) The world model they created monitored five trends of global concern—accelerating industrialization, rapid population growth, widespread malnutrition, depletion of nonrenewable resources, and a deteriorating environment.[33] They said these trends are all "interconnected in many ways, and their development is measured in decades or centuries, rather than in months or years."[34] They concluded the following:

1. If the present growth trends in world population, industrialization, pollution, food production, and resource depletion continue unchanged, the limits to growth on this planet would be reached sometime within the next one hundred years.

2. It is possible to alter these growth trends and to establish a condition of ecological and economic stability that is sus-

tainable far into the future. The state of global equilibrium could be designed so that the material needs of each person on earth are satisfied and each person has an equal opportunity to realize his individual human potential.

3. If the world's people decide to strive for this second outcome, rather than the first, the sooner they begin working to attain it, the greater their chances of success.[35]

Furthermore, these social, economic, and environmental planners called for every phase of each person's life to be planned. Perhaps our greatest example of what kind of Utopia they have in mind can be best seen by looking at some of the policies of China. The Club of Rome advocates "nongrowth" policies and suggests the following:

1. The population has access to one hundred percent effective birth control.
2. The average desired family size is two children.
3. The economic system endeavors to maintain average industrial output per capita at about the 1975 level.[36]

Lastly, they concluded that nongrowth policies have been advocated by others before them, such as Plato, Aristotle, and Thomas Robert Malthus.[37]

It should be noted that the year this landmark report was published, 1972, the United Nations held their first environmental conference, the United Nations Conference of the Human Environment. The policies stated above have been incorporated into all of the United Nations environmental and governmental policies which are advocated by both the Clinton administration and Prince Charles.

In the influential book, *Small Is Beautiful,* E. F. "Fritz" Schumacher wrote: "Human scale thinking must have a spiritual content. . . . We have to put back what our dominant industrialist–

materialist–scientific world view leaves out. The omitted area is what we mean by spiritual."[38]

The concept of sustainable development is spiritual and it does embrace the nongrowth policy. The "small is beautiful" concept is basically used with communities to keep them self-contained and provide a way for the state to monitor people, community by community.

In the interview with Dr. Wally N'Dow in March 1997, I asked him how Habitat II, held in June 1996, differed from the first Habitat Conference convened twenty years earlier. He replied:

In 1976, there were subjects that were taboo in the United Nations. One could not discuss subjects, such as the role of the private sector because we were still in the grips of the Cold War, with ideologies contending over what was capitalist, socialist, what was acceptable in the U.N. fora, and what could not be discussed—[like the] private sector and land—who owns it, how it is managed—these were the things that could not be discussed.

To put the philosophical difference into perspective, I followed up with a question on the difference (they appear to be the same) between the concept of community in the Habitat I document, and Habitat II, which is based on biospheres. His reply provides us with the reason as to why the community—the local level—is so important to those who want control:

Communities are the most important and primary agents of change in their own self management. It used to be that a lot of this was top down. . . . Today we are seeing a bottoms-up approach in terms of philosophy and in terms of effort [and] vision. So the community is the single most important unit that we have to deal with.

He went on to explain that community has another aspect, which is nonphysical: "Community spirit goes beyond those physical and tangible things. [It is] what keeps societies together."

What he means is that the environmental philosophy that the United Nations is espousing is the spirit that will keep communities together. If it is the corporations that are heralding this radical environmental agenda being pushed on the people of the world from the top down, then it is the corporations that will bring it in from the bottom up (where we live/work). When I was at the Habitat II Conference, they made it very clear that "everyone would have to participate in the community." I knew then that people would no longer have the freedom to choose. Unfortunately the day is coming *when individuals, like you, will have to choose how you are going to participate.* The stakes are very high—do you choose the United Nations and the environmental agenda your employer espouses, or do you choose the Constitution, which is based on the Bible? Your job is the price. Your personal holiness before God will provide you with the answer.

The Prince Working Behind World Scenes

Most people will not find Prince Charles or his environmental activities in the headlines of major newspapers. For example, as a means of pushing the radical United Nations environmental agenda to the forefront of the world's attention, Prince Charles held a two-day international seminar in April 1991 aboard the royal yacht *Britannia*, moored off the coast of Brazil. His goal was to bring together key international figures in an attempt to achieve a degree of harmony between the conflicting attitudes of Europe, the United States, and the developing nations (led by Brazil) over the United Nations' environmental agenda. Among others, he invited (then) Senator Albert Gore, senior officials from the World Bank, chief executives from companies such as Shell and British Petroleum, the principal nongovernmental organizations, and European politicians, including the British ministers of overseas aid and the environment.[39]

As mentioned, the first United Nations environmental conference was held in 1972 with the second one, the United Nations Conference on the Environment and Development (UNCED), held twenty years later. UNCED, also called the Earth Summit, was an unveiling of the philosophical shift from the Judeo-Christian world view to Gaia. The Programme of Action, called *Agenda 21*, is 297 pages long, and a second related document, *Global Biodiversity Assessment*, is over 1,100 pages long. Together these documents contain an agenda that can only be called evil, as the implementation of the action items will turn freedom into bondage and life into misery as all of what we know today will be replaced with a planned electronic society in which our only value will be to produce. This is the agenda Prince Charles is facilitating. In feudalistic times only the king and nobility owned land and had freedom. So, too, under United Nations rule, feudalistic times will return and the lights of freedom will go out. Charles has nothing to lose and the world to gain.

If Prince Charles is a prince only in title and heredity, and supposedly without any power, why then did he host a pre-conference of great magnitude, setting the tone for the Earth Summit held fourteen months later? Why did he not attend the conference with great fanfare, revealing his part?

The Common Mentor to Prince Charles

It should be noted that Vice-President Al Gore and Prince Charles have a common mentor, now-deceased oil industrialist Armand Hammer, who was godfather to Charles' firstborn son, Prince William. Armand Hammer, in his autobiography *Hammer*, tells how he met Prince Charles in 1977 at an exhibition of paintings and drawings by Sir Winston Churchill. He writes that the beginning of their "deeply cherished and wide-ranging friendship"[40] began when he offered to Charles one of Churchill's paintings for the Queen's Jubilee Fund. A year later the Prince invited Mr.

and Mrs. Hammer to a reception at Buckingham Palace for Friends of the United World Colleges (UWC). Since Hammer did not have any knowledge of the colleges, Prince Charles introduced him to his "great-uncle Lord Louis Earl Mountbatten of Burma and Britain's last Viceroy of India. Lord Louis had been the first President of the International Council of United World Colleges." Mountbatten went on to tell Hammer:

> I witnessed the horrors of two world wars, and I came to the conclusion that, if we were ever to have peace in the world, we would have to start with young people of an impressionable age who would learn to live together regardless of their nationality, or religion, or their ideology.[41]

Originated by Kurt Hahn, founder of Prince Charles's old school, Gordonstoun, and the Outward Bound survival programs, the United World Colleges were formed to provide education for the brightest of the world's young citizens. The first United World College opened in Wales, with additional colleges in Canada, Singapore, Italy, and Swaziland. Pushing aside existing roadblocks, it was Dr. Hammer who was able to facilitate the establishment of a UWC in the United States. In 1982, the Armand Hammer United World College of the American West opened its doors in Montezuma, New Mexico.[42] Prince Charles served as its president up until recently. Currently Queen Noor of Jordan and Nelson Mandela of South Africa serve as co-presidents.

The goal of the UWC is to instruct in peace studies, which are taught as part of the international baccalaureate, a six–subject diploma accepted as a university entrance qualification. The peace studies syllabus looks at issues on three levels: the individual, social, and international. Students are instructed in subjects such as the arms race, superpower conflict, and the theory and practice of non-violence.[43] Interestingly enough, the United Nations has these same goals.

It was Armand Hammer's father Julius who was active in

the American Socialist Labor Party, naming his son after the symbol of the Communist Party, the arm and hammer. By 1919 Julius was involved in "establishing the left-wing section of the Socialist Party of the United States [which] was an early beachhead in America, a revolutionary Leninist organization."[44] This was only the beginning of the Hammer family's dealings with Lenin and other communist leaders after him. Part of their fortune was made from selling grain and flour to the communists in exchange for concessions of Russian products, including art from the czar. In the United States, Hammer's company was the first of one hundred U.S. companies that would do business in Russia after the Communist Revolution.

Hammer had access to many American presidents, senators, and congressman to help further his cause and provide him with the contacts he needed to sell grain, fertilizers, and other American products to the Russians. Among the senators, however, Al Gore, Sr., was key, working endlessly to introduce Hammer to members of the Senate, a job which Vice-President Gore assumed when his father retired from the Senate to run one of Occidental Petroleum's coal companies, owned by Hammer.

It is noteworthy to point out that the top environmentalists in the United States and United Kingdom are Al Gore and Prince Charles. In 1966, Charles became a patron to Intermediate Technology (IT), an international nongovernmental organization that helps poor people lift themselves out of poverty through technology. In keeping with the ideas and concepts fostered by the President's Commission on Sustainable Development, IT is being promoted here in America.

Like Al Gore, Anthony Blair, the current prime minister of Britain is a close friend of Prince Charles, and supports his environmental beliefs. The prince, by using world leaders who are willing to sell their souls, is plunging the world into deep, deep, bondage. It is by the purity, holiness, and desire of the set-apart, discerning Christian, that we can bend back the line.

Chapter Four

Sustainable Development

A Paradigm Shift in
Values, Economics, and Governance

The environmental agenda is extremely complex. A few words or charts cannot even begin to help the unfamiliar reader fathom the depth, width, breadth, and height of this evil plan. First, let me state that most of us *are* basically concerned with recycling, clean water, and air. However, the environmental platform, for the most part, is fraught with inconsistencies and theories that cannot be proved and provide the UN the platform it needs to seize control of the earth's resources in order to "protect them." The cornerstone and over-arching concept of the environmental agenda, which is the expansion of the Gaia theory, is "sustainable development."

Sustainable development is like a prism. Every time you turn it, you get a different color. The sustainable development prism includes the social, political, economic, and environmental facets. It was the United Nations Conference on Environment and Development (UNCED), held in June 1992, that set the tone and provided the support for the philosophical shift to holism—earth over man. It was in Agenda 21, the UNCED Programme of Action, that the term "sustainable development" was first used. Before that time, it does not appear that it was used in any of the 1970s or 1980s United Nations documents or reference books.

It should be noted that Agenda 21 sets up the global infrastructure needed to manage, count, and control all of the world's assets. Included are the forests, fresh water, agricultural lands, deserts, pastures, rangelands, farmers' fields, oceans and inland waterways, marine environment, marine life, cities, housing, sewer and solid wastes, methods of production, air, pollution, biotechnology—every aspect of living—farming, production and manufacturing, research and medicine, etc., along with you and me. As a result of advanced technology through computers and satellites—the Geographic Information System (GIS)—the management, count, and control is being done.

In addition to sustainable development and holism, there were a number of major conventions that were agreed upon at the Earth Summit: the Convention on Biological Diversity (which puts holism into practice), the Convention on Desertification, and the Convention on Climate Change. If ratified by our Senate in any form, these conventions will change the freedoms we have known, the standard of living we have enjoyed, and our ability to choose what we think is best for our family and business. This is the agenda of Prince Charles, and therefore the United Nations.

With regard to the various facets of sustainable development, the effects of the social are most prominent. The tools for reducing the population include abortion, condom distribution, sex education, family planning, RU486, the encouragement of homosexuality (no procreation), and of course, "the right to die with dignity" for those who have outlived their productive lives. The environmental facet is seen in the quest for control of the earth's resources—gold, silver, copper, uranium, oil, gas, etc. The economic facet is evidenced in the new environmental processes for saving water, cleaning the air, recycling, etc. Businesses can increase profits as well as the need for new and special environmental equipment (e.g., equipment designed to clean the air of carbon dioxide emissions) that United States manufacturers have available for such an opportune time as this.

The Background History of Sustainable Development

The World Commission on Environment and Development

In 1972 the first United Nations Earth Summit was held in Stockholm, Sweden, where the environmental infrastructure was set in place. In 1974 the General Assembly called for the United Nations Environment Programme (UNEP), the International Union for Conservation of Nature and Natural Resources (IUCN), now called the World Conservation Union, and the World Wildlife Fund (WWF) to "develop guidelines to help Governments in the management of their living resources through the formulation of a world conservation strategy."[45] When it was finished in 1980, the aforementioned groups had also collaborated with the Food and Agricultural Organization of the United Nations (FAO) and the United Nations Educational, Scientific and Cultural Organization (UNESCO) to prepare the *World Conservation Strategy* (WCS).[46] "The *World Conservation Strategy* provides both an intellectual framework and practical guidance for the conservation actions necessary." Their aim is to "help advance the achievement of sustainable development through the conservation of living resources."[47] In April 1980 the WCS was endorsed by the General Assembly. (This action led to the radical Agenda 21 programme, which endorses sustainable development, unveiled at UNCED in 1992.)

In the fall of 1983, the 38th Session of the United Nations General Assembly passed Resolution 38/161, which called upon the secretary-general to appoint a commission "to propose long-term environmental strategies for achieving sustainable development to the year 2000 and beyond;"[48] among other goals.

The individuals chosen for that commission, called the World Commission on Environment and Development, were both present and past world leaders. Gro Harlem Brundtland, former prime minister of Norway and vice-president of the Socialist International, was co-chairman. As is always the case, Maurice Strong, secretary general of the first (1972) and second Earth Summit (1992), was an advisor. Most members who served on the commission, with the exception of the representative from the United States, William Ruckleshaus (who is a globalist in his politics), are socialist, Marxist, or communist, depending on the country they came from—Russia, China, Hungary, Germany, Japan, Nigeria, Yugoslavia, Guyana, Algeria, Zimbabwe, or the Sudan, to name a few of the countries[49] where personal property rights do not exist.

In addition to the members of the commission, there were about one thousand individuals, institutes, and organizations from all over the world that provided support by submitting papers for public hearings, as well as studies and comments. Fifty-one of the names were from the USSR, while some were from well-known environmental groups like Greenpeace International, World Wildlife Fund, Wildlife Federation, and Worldwatch Institute, to name a few. Two other names of interest are William K. Reilly, president of the Conservation Foundation, USA (and former secretary of EPA), and World Vision. [50]

Definition of Sustainable Development

The commission is given credit for developing the definition of sustainable development. This philosophy changes the current world order which has existed from the time of the Garden of Eden, to an old world order (Satan's world order has been around since he rebelled) now called the new world order, which is holism. Holism has been gaining popularity for at least the last one hundred and fifty years. With the adoption of sustainable development at UNCED, man was demoted to the same level as a plant or animal. The commission's definition of sustainable development is:

> Development that meets the needs of the present without compromising the ability of future generations to meet their own

needs. . . . two concepts: (1) Needs as it pertains to the world's poor to which overriding priority should be given, (2) the idea of limitations imposed by . . . technology . . . on the environment's ability to meet present and future needs. . . . At a minimum, sustainable development must not endanger the natural systems that support life on Earth: atmosphere, water, soils, living beings.[51]

Overpopulation

Let me provide for you my own paraphrased definition of sustainable development, which I think is simpler to understand and embraces all of their points: The world has too many people, and if we do not reduce the number of people on planet Earth they will use up all of the Earth's resources so that future generations will be left without any resources. The United Nations is the best global body to monitor, manage, and preserve the resources of the planet.

The concept of sustainable development is not to be found in any of the writings or theories of the United Nations or environmentalists before 1990, and specifically 1992, when the United Nations Conference on the Environment and Development (UNCED), also called the Earth Summit, was held in Rio de Janeiro. The United Nations held its first environmental conference in 1972 and, interestingly enough, the phrase was only used once, without definition. Since Rio, it has been widely heralded and discussed in all United Nations documents.

In order to set the tone for sustainable development to the people of the world, the United Nations has sponsored numerous mega-conferences. The first set was held in the 1970s with a very large infrastructure put in place at that time. The seven follow-up conferences of the 1990s began in 1992 with the Rio Earth Summit and ended with the World Food Summit in 1996. Each meeting highlighted a different aspect of sustainable development.

The theme at the 1994 United Nations Conference on Population and Development in Cairo (ICPD) was to reduce the population of the world. Participants pushed condom distribution, abortion (the Catholic Church fought abortion being used as a means of family planning, which is supposed to be in effect today), and family planning education on a worldwide basis to promote the need for a small family (the Club of Rome). In addition, the World Bank announced that in the future, when any country applies for a loan, that loan will only be given if that particular country can prove it is reducing the size of its population.

It should be noted that there is no problem with overpopulation. There are many scientists who have proven that overpopulation is a myth. Dr. Jacqueline Kasun from Hamboldt University is one of them. She proved statistically that if you were to take all of the people of the world and put them in one state, they would fit in the state of Texas. Please refer to her very fine book, *The War Against Population*.[52]

How is the population being reduced? Abortion, condom distribution, "family planning," homosexuality, euthanasia, wars, genocide, famine, and plagues.

As a community activist a number of years ago, I was concerned about these social ills and their advocacy by our school system. While I could surmise that they come down to the local level from the state and federal levels, it was not until I went to my first United Nations Conference on Population in Cairo that I understood where they originated—on the global level! The chart on the following page is one I compiled showing five of the seven United Nations conferences and their objectives, and how they affect us on the local level.

Sustainable development has been adopted not only by the United Nations, all of its global commissions and agencies, but by all of the population reduction groups, which include the Guttmacher Institute, American Association for the Advance of Science, the American Humanist Association, the Center for Popu-

What Is Happening on the Global Level Does Affect Us Below

1. **U.N. Conference on Environment and Development— "Earth Summit"**—Rio, June 1992
   The Environment—Agenda 21—*animals/earth above people*
2. **U.N. International Conference on Population and Development**—Cairo, September 1994
   The Environment and Population Control—*reduce population*
3. **The Social Summit**—Copenhagen, March 1995
   Environment, Population Control, Poverty, Unemployment, Social Disintegration—*real agenda: global tax, U.N. power*
4. **Fourth Women's Conference**—Beijing, September 1995
   Roll-up of ERA, U.N. Rights of Child, and CEDAW into one—*attacks U.S. sovereignty and endorses Marxist/Leninist economics on a global basis*
5. **Habitat II**—Istanbul, June 1996
   Puts in place the legal/economic structure for implementing the above conferences. Sustainable development=governance=public/private partnerships=one world

▼	▼	▼	▼	▼
Reduce Population	*Acceptance of Diversity*	*Empowerment of Women*	*Empowerment of U.N.*	*U.N. Structure*
Abortion rights for all countries	Homosexual rights	Women become equal producers/ partners	Loss of national sovereignty	Rule 61-63; solidarity; loss of property rights; redistribution of wealth; public/private partnerships

▼

United States

► *Concerns we are addressing:*

National	►	State	►	Local
abortion		abortion		abortion
condom distribution		condom distribution		condom distribution
drugs/euthanasia		drugs/euthanasia		drugs/euthanasia
FACE		FACE		FACE
OBE–Goals 2000		OBE–Goals 2000		OBE–Goals 2000
health care		health care		health care
pornography		pornography		pornography
RICO		RICO		RICO
RU486		RU486		RU486
homo/bi youth clubs		homo/bi youth clubs		homo/bi youth clubs

lation Options, the Population Council, the Rockefeller Foundation, Advocates for Youth, SEICUS, and Zero Population Growth, to name a few. Two of the more well-known organizations are Planned Parenthood Federation of America and its counterpart, International Planned Parenthood. Their *Vision 2000* report supports the "links between population and sustainable development."[53]

Needless to say, the Clinton Administration has embraced the United Nations agenda, and this is what we are up against today—a very mighty, evil, global agenda.

The Philosophy of Sustainable Development

Where does sustainable development come from? Before I went to the June 1996 UN Conference on Human Settlements (Habitat II) in Istanbul, I was trying to determine its origin. The number of people serving on the World Commission on Environment and Development who were communist, Marxist, or socialist provided my first clue. In thinking about that, it occurred to me that this philosophy is not in our Constitution. I then looked in a constitution opposite of ours, the constitution of the Union of Soviet Socialist Republics (1977). I found my answer in Chapter 2, Article 18, which states:

> In the interests of the present and future generations, the necessary steps are taken in the USSR to protect and make scientific, rational use of the land and its mineral and water resources, and the plant and animal kingdoms to preserve the purity of air and water, ensure reproduction of natural wealth, and improve the human environment.[54]

In the executive summary of the book *Business as Partners in Development: Creating Wealth for Countries, Companies and Communities,* the authors write: "In most cases, the debate is no longer about extreme alternatives—about communism versus capitalism, the free market versus state control, democracy versus dictatorship—but about finding common good."[55]

Family Dependency Ratio

In order to understand the hidden evil and control of sustainable development, we need to look at two of the many ways in which the United Nations is working to "conserve and preserve the earth's resources": family dependency ratio and private property rights.

While researching the Fourth Women's Conference document, I stumbled across a new phrase, "family dependency ratio."[56] Since the United Nations does not define its terms, I came up with my own as a result of reading the rest of the document. I have to admit it was very "Orwellian." While at the Gorbachev State of the World Forum in October 1995, I was able to ask Maurice Strong, secretary-general of the United Nations' first and second environmental conferences and special advisor to Secretary General Kofi Annan and James Wolfensohn (president of the World Bank), if I was correct, and he verified that I was. The family dependency ratio basically monitors how many nonproducing members of a family are dependent on the producing family members. In order not to use up the earth's resources, the United Nations wants to monitor how much of the earth's resources each household is using.

The World Bank and United Nations are looking to measure how much each household in the world consumes, and how much of the earth's resources it produces. For example, if a household has four people, Mom and Dad work and produce, while the baby and grandparent do not produce (they consume). The World Bank is currently working on a way to assign a value to production, both at work and at home (e.g., cleaning and improving the house, educating yourself, volunteering in the community). What is consumed is then deducted from the total produced at work and at home to see if a household is adding to, or taking away from, the earth's resources. Volunteerism will have an entirely different meaning when you have to put back the resources you used from the earth.

Monitoring Our Assets

In 1993, the World Bank established a division for sustainable development. The World Bank has since added four other dimensions for monitoring the assets of the world through sustainable development. They are:

1. Natural capital—the minerals of the earth, water, forests, anything natural.
2. Manufactured capital—anything built, such as roads, buildings, homes, etc.
3. Human capital—every living person on the earth, including their age, health, experience, education, and ability to work.
4. Social capital—how people think, that is, politically correct thinking.

The World Bank and the IMF for the most part have developed, or are in the process of developing, how to measure each of these in every country, including the United States. All United Nations and United Nations-related organizations and agencies espouse sustainable development. These concepts permeate UN documents, goals, seminars, and pilot projects, and are coming to your house soon.

Since *Our Common Future* was published, sustainable development has quickly been adopted by local, state, and federal governmental levels in all countries, and by multinational corporations. Sustainable development has been incorporated not only into the whole philosophy of the United Nations and their mega-conferences throughout the 1990s, but by the International Chamber of Commerce (which filters down to the local level), the World Bank and all of its lending practices, the International Monetary Fund, and many other global groups and organizations as well. Here in the United States, President Clinton established by executive order in 1993 the President's Commission on Sustainable Development (PCSD), which has added this dimension to most, if not all, federal levels of government without the consent of Congress. The PCSD has announced a national conference on sustainable development to be held May 2–5, 1999, in Detroit. Support for this conference comes from the U.S. Conference of Mayors and the National Association of Counties.

Public-Private Partnerships—
The Result of Sustainable Development

The vehicle to enforce the concept of sustainable development is the public-private partnership. The diagram on the next page, "Multi-Stakeholder Partnership,[57]" diagrams this interconnectedness, which mirrors Charles's holistic philosophy and that of the environmental agenda. The government, private business, and civil society are one. This also is referred to as "governance" which the United Nations defines as "the exercise of political, economic and administrative authority in the management of a country's affairs at all levels."[58] (These are components of public–private partnerships; therefore, public-private partnership and governance are also one.) The United Nations has many different forms of governance—global governance, corporate governance, governance for sustainable human development, etc. Please refer to the chapter on governance.

This interconnectedness has been reinforced in a number of conferences that I have attended. At the Fifth Annual World Bank Conference on Environmentally and Socially Sustainable Development in October 1997, panelist Carolyn McAskie said:

Multi-Stakeholder Partnership
Building Bridges Towards Sustainable Development

One of the major challenges facing the world community as it seeks to replace unsustainable development patterns with environmentally sound and sustainable development, is the need to activate a sense of common purpose on behalf of all sectors of society. The chances of forging such a sense of purpose will depend on the willingness of all sectors to participate in genuine social partnership and dialogue, while recognising the independent roles, responsibilities and special capacities of each.

Chapter 27, Agenda 21

Agenda 21 addresses the pressing problems of today and also aims to prepare the world for the challenges of the next century. It reflects a global consensus on development and environment cooperation. Its successful implementation is first and foremost the responsibility of governments.

Preamble, Chapter 1, Agenda 21

(Political)
GOVERNMENT
- National, state, local
- Multilateral and bilateral governmental organisations.

(Economic)
PRIVATE SECTOR/BUSINESS
- Corporations and multinationals
- Business and industry associations
- Small and micro enterprises

(Social)
CIVIL SOCIETY NON-GOVERNMENTAL/ ORGANISATIONS
- NGOs are diverse and multi-faceted, their perspectives and operations may be:
  –Local, national, regional, or global
  –Issue, task, or ideology oriented
  –Broad public interest or private
  –Small, poorly funded grassroots to large, professionally staffed bodies
  –Individual or networked

Business and industry, including transnational corporations and their representative organisations, should be full participants in the implementation and evaluation of activities related to Agenda 21.

Strengthening the Role of Business and Industry, Chapter 30, Agenda 21

Non-governmental organisations play a vital role in the shaping and implementation of participatory democracy. Their credibility lies in the responsible and constructive role they play in society. Formal and informal organisations, as well as grass-roots movements, should be recognised as patterns in the implementation of Agenda 21.

Strengthening the Role of NGOs, Chapter 27, Agenda 21

The theme of this conference is a critical one. Partnerships, links, and connections both within and among the countries of the world. [K]nowledge for sustainable development . . . is the essential building block of development. Sustainable development demands partnerships. The ultimate partnership of the decade has been the global treaties, and conventions [which] not only bind nations together to work toward common objectives . . . they promote and guide international cooperation."[59]

This same interconnectedness can be seen in the merging of environment, economics, and social issues into one. This was the theme of Hillary Clinton's speech in February 1998 at the World Economic Forum. This is another aspect of the public-private partnership concept. As the environmental ideology permeates all aspects of life, it takes on a spiritual dimension that mirrors the Gaia philosophy, which is paganism. When the three become one through partnership, they form a philosophical approach that will change representative government in America. As the precepts of the Constitution are eliminated through new (United Nations-policy guided) legislation, the power of the Constitution is eroded and in its place are public-private partnerships which run parallel to representative government and form the new governance for the twenty-first century. This is a new twist to the concept of world government that most people visualize, and is the key to understanding how important the Prince of Wales is, and the corporations to which he is providing leadership.

Through public-private partnerships, the balance of power shifts from the people to the partner who has the most money. This is, and always will be, man's way of acquiring power. As the power shifts to the deepest pockets (the corporation), we have then moved into fascism—rule by big (reinvented) government and big business. Note: Reinvented government refers to: (1) the downsizing of federal government in order to fit into the future global governance scheme as outlined in the chapter on "The

Empowerment of the United Nations," and (2) the government's shift to privatization of public services through public-private partnerships.

All across America, public-private partnerships are being established that solidify the government/corporation as ruler. A number of organizations are facilitating this change, including: the National Council for Public-Private Partnerships, Washington, D.C.; the National Civic League, located in Denver, Colorado, whose president is former United States Senator Bill Bradley, a Rhodes Scholar; and KPMG (PWBLF council member), who provides advice for public-private partnerships in a number of areas. Targeted industries for the public-private partnership takeover include: water supply, sanitation, and electricity.

For example, I read recently where the city of Seattle needs a new sewer system which they estimate will cost $650 million through raising taxes. I would anticipate that a "public-private partnership" will be formed that will involve one of the large multinational corporations domiciled in Washington State along with local and state government. In Indiana, the White River Environmental Partnership was formed which is under contract with the city of Indianapolis to manage and operate the city's two wastewater facilities and its sewer collection system. This is the largest contract of its kind in the United States and is a public–private partnership. United Water, which is located in New Jersey, forms public-private partnerships with many municipalities across the United States for water and wastewater management. Look around your community. You will be shocked to discover the number of public-private partnerships that have "popped up" in the last five to ten years.

In summary, the word "sustainable" represents "control," which means different laws are needed to change and transcend national laws. On January 15, 1998, Vice-President Al Gore, in commenting on the frozen blizzard in Maine, told the citizens the federal government would do "everything possible as their *partner."* As Bill Clinton said in his 1997 inaugural address, we need a

> new sense of responsibility for a new century. With a *new* vision of government, a *new* sense of responsibility, a *new* spirit of community, we will sustain America's journey. The promise we sought in a *new* land we will find again in a land of *new* promise.[60] (emphasis added)

What the President did not specify is that this "new land" would be one in which representative government and our freedoms will be changed to conform with the type of governance found in the U.N. charter. It appears all roads lead to England.

Chapter 5

Global Governance

Public-Private Partnerships and
Governance are ONE

It is on the global level that a number of key concepts and philosophies come together. Charles has adopted a very radical environmental agenda that calls for a planned society, using the environment and sustainable development as the reason for the change in governance (government) and freedoms. Public-private partnerships are the *modus operandi* to effect this change. The definition of governance by the UNDP (chapter four) is that public–private partnerships and governance (government) are one. In other words, sustainable development equals governance equals public-private partnerships equals ONE (government). We will be controlled, on the local from the global through public-private partnerships, bypassing the federal and state levels, rendering them obsolete.

The Prince of Wales Business Leaders Forum works very closely with the United Nations Development Programme (UNDP) and the World Bank as well as a number of other multilateral and global agencies and organizations. The executive director of the UNDP is James Gustave Speth, who has held very important and key positions in a number of key radical environmental groups. In 1982 he was chosen to head the World Resources Institute, which was created by the International Union for the Conservation of Nature (IUCN). Appointed by Bill Clinton,

Speth's term will end about the time Al Gore runs in 1999. When I attended the Rio+5 conference in March 1997, Mr. Speth delivered what can only be called an important keynote speech on sustainable development and the role of both state and nonstate actors in global governance. He said:

Let me emphatically state that global governance is not global government, but a set of interacting guidance and control mechanisms that include both state (public) and nonstate (private) actors, actors both public and private, both national and multilateral. Global governance is here, here to stay, and driven by economic and environmental globalization. Global governance has coexisted for many years with strong, sovereign states. International arrangements, such as the Rhine and Danube Commissions, existed since the early years of the nineteenth century to oversee transport on major rivers.

They were joined in the second part of the nineteenth century by such agencies as the International Telecommunications Union (1865), the World Meteorological Organization (1873), the Universal Postal Union (1875)—a precursor to the International Organization for Standardization—the World Intellectual Property Organization (1883), [and] the International Rail Transport Organization in 1880. In the early years of the twentieth century, the World Health Organization and the International Labour Organization (1919) were created. Each of these institutional innovations and the resulting international regulation reflect the reality that economic and other needs spur global governance.

Today the system of global governance is undergoing a profound transformation. At the qualitative level, nonstate actors, mainly NGOs [nongovernmental organizations] and businesses, have seen their influence increase in global governance. Nor are NGOs the only nonstate actors to participate in the evolution of global governance mechanisms. The phenomenal growth of multinational enterprise is a potent force in the global governance. The presence here of Klaus Schwab [founder and president of the World Economic Forum] and Stephan Schmidheiny and his colleagues with the World Business Council for Sustainable Development is ample evidence of this.

Just as important, we look forward to a *growing role in supporting the involvement and participation of NGOs and civil society organizations, including private business, in forging partnerships of many types—partnerships [public-private] that are an integral part of the web of global governance and the glue that holds our troubled world together.*

(emphasis added)

From Speth's speech, we can see that the combination of partnerships plus governance equals one (government). While rumor has it that Speth will either head up Gore's election campaign or possibly be considered for the position of vice-president, one wonders, after working so closely with Prince Charles, where Speth's loyalties will really lie.

Governance from the Global to the Local
At the Habitat II Conference in Istanbul (see chapter six), the United Nations opened the doors for mayors to directly affect the formulation of United Nations policy through Committee 2. What this really does is eliminate, or bypass, the state and federal levels in favor of local levels which will carry out the United Nations agenda.

In July 1997 the United Nations held the International Conference on Governance for Sustainable Growth and Equity. The purpose of this conference was to provide a forum for representatives of governments, parliaments, local authorities, civil society, and United Nations agencies to share the best practices in governance for sustainable growth which includes sustainable human development. The various forums held simultaneously were for: ministerial/senior officials; mayors; parliamentarians; and civil society.

The Prince of Wales Business Leaders Forum participated in the forum for mayors and the forum for civil society. According to independent journalist Linda Liotta who attended the conference, "the secretary-general opened the meeting by telling participants that, 'You are the agents of change and of a new politics' and that '[g]ood governance and sustainable development are indivisible.'"

She told me:

> The U.N. brought in the local level from around the world. For the first time in U.N. history, the opening and closing conference ceremonies were held in the General Assembly giving special rights and recognition to the local level. The participants sat in the places where the appointed U.N. ambassadors to the UN sit.

Two American mayors attended. San Francisco mayor Willie Brown said: "I am delighted and honored . . . to participate in this very necessary conference. . . . Cities are going to be where people actually live. Cities are going to be where policies of the UN, as well as the federal government, will ultimately be implemented."

Seattle mayor Norman Rice said: "Sustainability today requires communities to constantly work toward a strong future through partnerships between government, business, labor, and the citizenry."

Lastly, the UNDP which partners with the Prince of Wales Business Leaders Forum, produced a policy paper in which director James Gustave Seph wrote: "We aim to be an impartial partner to governments, to civil society, and to the private sector. . . ."[61] The paper states, "UNDP devotes one- third of their resources for governance" and "only recently became involved with legislative and judicial systems."[62]

State of Maryland Adopts Public-Private Partnerships
In an interview with Baltimore Mayor Kurt Schmoke in March 1997, at the Maryland State House where he was lobbying for two bills that would set up public-private partnerships, I asked him the following questions:

Veon: Some people are concerned about personal property rights. . . . Do you see that as a problem?

Mayor: No, I don't think so. I don't think there is any intention to undermine personal property rights, but I think like all rights that we have, there has to be some compromise because individual rights run up against collective rights. . . . The local prerogatives . . . will have to be compromised to a certain extent to deal with the greater good.

Veon: Then do you see collectivism as the new wave for the twenty-first century?

Mayor: I would prefer to call it partnership—I think that's better—it's "partners in progress" and that is what the governor is trying to achieve, and I support him.

Veon: Public-private partnerships?

Mayor: Correct.

Chapter 6

The Empowerment of the United Nations

Introduction

In order to understand the power which Charles has, we must look at the increased strength of both the United Nations and transnational corporations. It is not enough to state "Charles is powerful," one must explain how he is powerful in order to understand the magnitude of the day and the hour. Not only is the Rhodes legacy complete through the United Nations, but the apex of the global governmental structure is being revealed through his actions and activities.

At the Gorbachev State of the World Forum in October 1995, which I attended, Zbigniew Brezezinski, former national security advisor under President Carter and director of the Trilateral Commission, said:

> Finally, I have no illusions about world government emerging in our life time . . . [through] a process of gradually expanding the range of democratic cooperation as well as the range of personal and national security. A widening, step by step, stone by stone . . . [through] genuine globalization, [which] is progressive regionalization.

This widening is being done specifically through the empowerment of the United Nations system. Empowerment comes as a result of environmental treaties and conventions to which the countries of the world (somehow) give their consent. This then requires an expansion on the part of the United Nations to operate and monitor how the countries are implementing the new agreements. Without the mantra of the environment, the United Nations would have no reason for expansion and empowerment.

U.N. Studies Calling for U.N. Empowerment

There are two very similar studies calling for the same kind of expansion: *Renewing the United Nations System* and *Our Global Neighborhood*. They both recommend expanding the Security Council and eliminating the veto; adding a Sustainable Development Division or expanding the Trusteeship Council to monitor the "global commons" that we share (atmosphere, outer space, the oceans beyond national jurisdiction, etc.);[63] and to monitor the progress of countries adopting sustainable development goals, adding an Economic Security Council, and giving the World Bank and International Monetary Fund vast powers over the world's economic system. A longstanding recommendation has been to add a "People's Assembly." This call dates back to a speech that Ernest Bevin, foreign secretary of the U.K., made before the General Assembly where he called for "a world assembly elected directly from the people of the world to whom the governments who form the United Nations are responsible."[64]

Note: Any world elections will be based on a country's population, which automatically gives India and China a greater number of representatives. See Appendix A for update.

While I was aware of a number of recommendations, I had a call several months ago from a researcher in Wisconsin who excitedly told me he had found a 1988 chart showing the "future United Nations." I quickly acquired the book and immediately saw the planned infrastructure in the "New Models of Governance" chart, which is reprinted with the permission of Gaia Publishing Ltd., London, England.

"New Models of Governance"

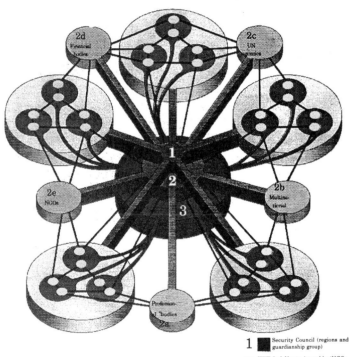

1	■	Security Council (regions and guardianship group)
2	■	2nd Upper Assembly (NGOs, peoples)
3	■	1st Lower Assembly (States)
	▦	Transnational bodies
	▨	Regions
	■	States
	□	Communities

The black lines appear to symbolize the electronic connection in the world through the Internet.

Published by: Gaia Publishing Lmt., London.
Used by permission.

Although it may appear to be complex, it is extremely important. When we consider exactly *what* the prince is doing, we must also understand the *depth*. Public-private partnerships have two major players: government and corporations. The UN is trying to acquire greater power in a number of ways which includes the People's Assembly, while corporations are trying to pass the controversial Multilateral Agreement on Investments (see chapter seven). Put Prince Charles at the helm and you have a very complete picture. The only entities that will be sustainable are the corporations and the UN.

"New Models of Governance"

Currently the UN is comprised of the (#1) Security Council and (#3) the First Lower Assembly (States). Veteran internationalist Maurice Strong suggests that we need "a bicameral system in which directly-elected representatives of peoples sit in one chamber and representatives of government in the other."[65]

The chart shows several levels of governance: (1) the Security Council, (2) the Upper Chamber or People's Assembly, and (3) the Lower Chamber or General Assembly. Numbers have been added to the chart along with organizational names which will then provide you with a greater description of what I believe the chart means.

(1) Security Council

The five spokes coming from the Security Council, which is the hub, pertain to the five regions of the world. They also symbolize "regionalism." The United States has been under the rule of regionalism primarily since the thirties. It was Franklin Roosevelt who recommended this change. Currently, America is divided up into ten regions, while the world is divided into five. If you are going to have world government, you then need a way to govern the world more effectively. Regional divisions are a smaller way to handle an area. From there you go down to the communities, bypassing federal and state government, which will become obsolete in time. Currently a number of American states are trying to pass legislation to erase county government.

The nation-states appear to be under the control of the United Nations. Perhaps this is a way of showing the elimination of national governments. The vice-president's plan to "reinvent government" is part of a program to decentralize the federal government and move government down to the community level so that it is the global level directing the local level.

(2) 2nd Upper Assembly or "People's Assembly"

The move to add a second assembly to the United Nations has been gaining momentum. Many feel it is already in operation as indicated by my interview with Mayor Kurt Schmoke (below). Those who would represent you and me at the United Nations would be the currently accredited organizations that are already affiliated with the United Nations. Let us take a closer look.

In preparation for the 1996 Habitat II Conference held in Istanbul, the UN General Assembly passed Rules 61, 62, and 63 in December 1995. Boutros Boutros-Ghali termed this legislation as "historic" in that it set up Committee 2 and provided a way in which the world's mayors, scientists, businessmen, professionals, researchers, foundations, parliamentarians, labor unions, and nongovernmental organizations could directly impact the deliberations over and the preparation of UN policy as it took place in the plenary (congressional) sessions. (See the chart on the following page.) Committee 2 is, in essence, the "People's Assembly."

Baltimore mayor Kurt Schmoke, a Rhodes Scholar, was on the U.S. delegation in Istanbul along with two other mayors from the United States. I asked him what his presence meant. He replied in part:

> Well, what I have tried to do here is to let other members of the delegation and those from around the world know how impor-

The Anatomy of Habitat

"The U.N. Conference of Partners"

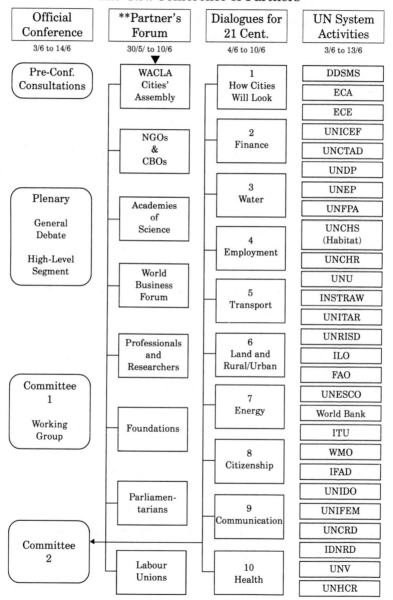

Official Conference	**Partner's Forum	Dialogues for 21 Cent.	UN System Activities
3/6 to 14/6	30/5/ to 10/6	4/6 to 10/6	3/6 to 13/6
Pre-Conf. Consultations	WACLA Cities' Assembly	1 How Cities Will Look	DDSMS
			ECA
			ECE
	NGOs & CBOs	2 Finance	UNICEF
			UNCTAD
			UNDP
Plenary	Academies of Science	3 Water	UNEP
General Debate			UNFPA
		4 Employment	UNCHS (Habitat)
High-Level Segment	World Business Forum		UNCHR
		5 Transport	UNU
			INSTRAW
			UNITAR
	Professionals and Researchers	6 Land and Rural/Urban	UNRISD
			ILO
			FAO
Committee 1		7 Energy	UNESCO
			World Bank
Working Group	Foundations		ITU
		8 Citizenship	WMO
			IFAD
	Parliamen-tarians	9 Communication	UNIDO
			UNIFEM
			UNCRD
Committee 2			IDNRD
	Labour Unions	10 Health	UNV
			UNHCR

**The Partner's Forum, in essence, constitutes the "People's Forum." They now have direct input into U.N. documents through Committee 2.

Source: Press Kit, Habitat II

tant this conference is to mayors in the United States. We just wanted people to know how important this conference is. It is the beginning of a new era with local government officials being listened to in the development of United Nations documents and we see this as kind of the wave of the future.

Just as local chamber of commerce chapters receive direction from the International Chamber of Commerce, so too, are mayors now conforming to the UN Charter.

Each one of the spokes coming from the 2nd Upper Assembly, or People's Assembly, represent entities that are currently active in supporting, implementing, and overseeing many of the policies of the United Nations, specifically with regard to the environment. They are:

2a—Professional Bodies

While there are numerous organizations which are active on the global level, the following are provided for your consideration:

Parliamentarians for Global Action (PGA). Parliamentarians for Global Action was begun in 1977 and is an international political network with over twelve hundred members drawn from eighty-five national legislatures. The goal of the organization is to promote international peace, security, democracy, and development through global cooperation and the strengthening of international institutions, treaties, and law. The PGA has sent delegates to observe transitional elections and to mediate political stalemates. It fosters multilateral cooperation among political leaders and has established a partnership with the World Bank. The organization also has had the support of a number of United States elected officials: Congressman James Leach served on its executive committee from 1989 to 1995; Rep. Gary Ackerman has served as a member-at-large with Senator Tom Harkin as a vice-chair; and Congresswoman Constance Morella from Maryland is a member. PGA is funded by the Carnegie Corporation,

Ford Foundation, MacArthur Foundation, and the Rockefeller Foundation, as well as various United Nations agencies and governments.[66]

World Economic Forum (WEF). The World Economic Forum is a not-for-profit foundation that acts as a "bridge builder between business and government." Its motto is: "Entrepreneurship in the global public interest." Yearly it brings one thousand corporate members from among the world's most successful global companies together with world leaders and members of the global community to encourage direct interaction between the public and private sectors for the purpose of creating a partnership committed to improving the state of the world.

The composition of participants at the 1998 WEF included eight members of the Trilateral Commission, forty-four members of the CFR, three who are members of both, sixty-nine with a past or current UN affiliation, nine Fulbright/Rhodes Scholars, and eight from the Royal Institute for International Affairs which endeavors to carry out the Rhodes legacy in reuniting America with Britain.

In 1992, the WEF acted as an official advisor to the Earth Summit in Rio; and in 1994, brought together Shimon Peres and PLO chairman Yasser Arafat, which started the Middle East peace talks. The WEF participated at the Rio+5 conference, sponsored by the Earth Council and chaired by Mikhail Gorbachev and Maurice Strong in March 1997.[67]

Foundations. Most of the leading United Nations nongovernmental organizations derive their funding from the major foundations. Over and over again, when you read an annual report or a brochure from those foundations in the NGO section, you will find the names of the John D. Rockefeller, Pew Charitable Trust, MacArthur, Ford, and Carnegie foundations. Without funding from these groups, the environmentalists and those looking to reduce the population would not have a chance with mainstream America!

2b—Multinational Corporations

When I interviewed Dr. Noel Brown, former director of UNEP, in March 1997 in Rio de Janeiro, he said with regard to public–private partnerships and a second UN chamber:

> I believe that the future of the United Nations will rest on effective partnering with the private sector—with business and industry. [A]s we look at . . . future [United Nations] revitalization . . . the success of the United Nations will depend on the success by which it brings in new powerholders of the world. I . . . see the United Nations with a new chamber for the industrial community. I would advise the secretary-general tomorrow to create a cooperative advisory council. He must have around him the top business leaders . . . and we need to create a second chamber for the United Nations.

While I never reported this, I was hoping it would never come to pass. However, I was sent a copy of an Internet correspondence which basically says the drive to add a second chamber (including business) is in the making.

The following is a message from Dr. David C. Korten, president of the PDC Forum. I think it would be fair to say that Mr. Korten is a New Ager and a staunch socialist. However, he is concerned about how people would really be treated in the evolving new world order. I interviewed him in 1996 for over an hour, and was shocked when he verbalized a number of my own thoughts. The following are excerpts from his Internet message:

> On June 24, 1997, the CEOs of ten TNCs [transnational corporations] met over lunch at the United Nations with the United Nations leadership and a number of senior government officials to chart a formalization of corporate involvement in the affairs of the United Nations. I attended the lunch. I found it a shattering experience, for it revealed a seamless alliance be-

tween the public and private sectors aligned behind the consolidation of corporate rule over the global economy. . . .

Thirty-seven invited participants were co-hosted by . . . the President of the United Nations General Assembly, and Mr. Bjorn Stigson, Executive Director of the World Business Council on Sustainable Development to examine steps toward establishing terms of reference for business sector participation in the policy-setting process of the United Nations and partnering in the uses of United Nations development assistance funds. [Korten describes some of the power members: the ICC and the ten CEOs who were members of the World Business Council for Sustainable Development, as well as those who represented business at the Rio Earth Summit.]

The meeting's outcome was preordained. . . . The President of the General Assembly, announce[d] that a framework for the involvement of the corporate sector in United Nations decision making would be worked out under the auspices of the Commission on Sustainable Development.

The International Chamber of Commerce (ICC). Founded in 1919 by a group of international businessmen, the ICC represents seventy-five hundred businesses and associations in one hundred thirty countries around the world. As a group, they supported the creation of the United Nations in 1945, regional government or "New Federalism," Medicare, the voucher system for education, federal land use planning, the Equal Rights Amendment, and now sustainable development. They have endorsed many of the United Nations environmental agreements and conventions and are working to get them ratified. National and local chamber chapters are found throughout the United States and usually vote the way the international organizations instructs them. The ICC operates on the global level with governments, businesses, and international organizations to further the goals of the United Nations. They have consultative status with the

Economic and Social Council (ECOSOC) of the United Nations. The International Chamber of Commerce, along with the World Business Council for Sustainable Development, would comprise the second assembly.[68]

The World Business Council for Sustainable Development (WBCSD). The World Business Council for Sustainable Development is a coalition of one hundred twenty international companies from thirty-four countries and more than twenty major business sectors who are concerned about economic growth and sustainable development. The WBCSD was formed in January 1995 through a merger between the Business Council for Sustainable Development in Geneva, and the World Industry Council for the Environment (WICE) in Paris. WICE was originally established by the United Nations Environment Programme.

The World Business Council for Sustainable Development promotes business leadership, policy development, best practice, and has a global outreach. Its aims are "to develop closer cooperation between business, government, and all other organizations concerned about the environment and sustainable development." Member companies include ABB (Asea Brown Boveri), AT&T, British Petroleum, DAN Hotels, Dow Chemical, DuPont, Eastman Kodak, Fiat, Hitachi, Itochu, James D. Wolfenson (the company), Johnson Matthey, Monsanto, Norsk Hydro, S. C. Johnson & Son, Shell International, Texaco, 3M, Tokyo Electric Power, Volkswagen, Waste Management International, and Xerox, to name several. Its current chairman is Livio DeSimone from 3M, and its executive director is Bjorn Stigson.[69]

2c—United Nations Agencies

There are four major specialized UN agencies: the International Labor Organization (ILO), the World Health Organization (WHO), the Food and Agriculture Organization (FAO), and the United Nations Educational, Scientific and Cultural Organization (UNESCO). Also with a number of specialized, technical agencies, such as the International Civil Aviation Organization, the World Meteorological Organization, and the Universal Postal Union.[70]

2d—Financial Bodies

The World Bank (WB). The World Bank plays a major role in lending to third world countries, developing the stock markets of emerging markets, issuing global bonds on the global market, supporting sustainable development, and many other activities.

The International Monetary Fund (IMF). Currently the IMF has strict rules and regulations for bringing the economics of a country into line. They have been realizing the economic growth of the countries of the world since 1944, reducing America's and increasing the economic growth of lesser developed countries like China and Vietnam.

The IMF had been realigning the economic growth of the countries of the world since 1944. America's economic growth has been gradually reduced and transferred to other countries which include Japan, China, and Vietnam. The IMF is known for their financial bail-outs of countries in distress. In exchange, the country must bring all of their financial systems under the direction of the IMF, which then commandeers what a country can do.

The International Organization of Security Commissions (IOSCO). The International Organization of Security Commissions was begun in the early seventies and is considered the "United Nations of Security Commissions." The United States Security and Exchange Commission was instrumental in setting up this strategic world body which monitors and regulates the securities and exchanges of each country in the world.

Note: Space doesn't permit a thorough explanation of the deep tentacles of each of these organizations and the role they play in globalization. I have written extensively about these groups in my economic newsletter, available through Veon Financial Services, Inc. (Please see my bio.)

2e—NGOs

Nongovernmental organizations can be divided up into two primary groups: environmental and population reduction. There are thousands upon thousands of these organizations all over the world. They are set up as nonprofits, and most of them have special recognition at the UN. Three of the very prominent environmental groups are mentioned below. Population reduction groups include the Sexuality Information and Education Council of the U.S. (SEICUS), International Planned Parenthood Federation, and the Women's Environment and Development Organization.

The World Conservation Union. The World Conservation Union, formerly the International Union for Conservation of Nature and Natural Resources (IUCN), was founded in 1948. This organization has more than eight hundred fifty members, including states, government agencies, and nongovernmental organizations. Its goals are to save endangered plant and animal species, create national parks and other protected areas, and assess the status of ecosystems in order to restore them. The IUCN is a major mover and shaker in the environmental movement. It has spearheaded a number of major environmental changes in the world, specifically the *World Conservation Strategy* (WCS), which was prepared in 1980 in cooperation with the United Nations Environment Programme and the World Wildlife Fund (WWF). This major work was the beginning of sustainable development and Agenda 21 (which was presented in Rio in 1992.) In addition to the World Conservation Strategy, the IUCN has published a number of very key environmental publications that are considered foundational building blocks for the new world order including *Caring for the Earth* and *From Care to Action—Making a Sustainable World.* IUCN credits the World Conservation Strategy as being commissioned by the United Nations Environmental Programme with financial support from both UNEP and the World Wildlife Fund. It has agreements with the World Bank, UNEP, and the Earth Council. Needless to say, the IUCN is not in favor of national sovereignty. Its roots go back to England.

World Resources Institute (WRI). With goals very similar to the others, the World Resources Institute receives great sums of money from the MacArthur Foundation, Andrew K. Mellon Foundation, and the Rockefeller Brothers Fund to conserve land. The current president is Jonathan Lash, who is cochairman of the President's Council on Sustainable Development. Past president James Gustave Speth, a Rhodes Scholar, is the Clinton appointee to the United Nations Development Fund and was quoted earlier.[71]

The Nature Conservancy (TNC). Founded in 1951, the Nature Conservancy has a membership of 708,000 individuals and 405 corporations. According to Ron Arnold and Alan Gottlieb of the Wiseuse Movement, it is the "Number One Economy Trasher" in the United States and the richest, with assets of $855 million. It raises funds and sells subscriptions. The Nature Conservancy makes a practice of buying private land and then selling it to "the federal government at a substantial mark up." They own five million acres of land in America, and twenty million in Latin America. The Nature Conservancy is credited with destroying thousands of jobs in America in order to protect land, which it ends up holding or selling for a profit. Land they bought is usually through surrogates who don't reveal the real purchaser. In 1979, the Nature Conservancy purchased an entire town.[72]

(3) First Lower Assembly (States)

Since 1945 in the General Assembly, or the Lower Assembly, is where the representatives of the countries of the world, who are members of the United Nations, meet. You will recall that the original purpose of the United Nations was to provide a forum where the countries of the world could talk out their differences. Indeed, the real purposes of the United Nations have been made very clear—peace was the *modus operandi* for world government. Through the environmental agenda, via sustainable development and public-private partnerships, a complete shift in philosophy and government has taken place. The empowerment of the United Nations is not by accident, nor is the empowerment of corporations or the fact that Charles heads up the Prince of Wales Business Leaders Forum.

Internet and the Electronic Society

If I had seen the "New Models of Governance" chart in 1988, I would not have known what the black lines were. However, with the advent of the Internet, it is quite clear that we are a wired society. It is the Group of Seven who has pushed for the Internet system and advanced technology. Today it appears that all of the transactions of life are being shifted to this electronic form of commerce which also has the ability to control and monitor users.

Chapter Seven

Facism and the Empowerment of Corporations

Fascism

While most of us are vaguely familiar with communism and socialism, we don't really know what "fascism" means.

The term comes from the Latin, *fasces,* meaning "a bundle of rods with an axe," the symbol of state power carried ahead of the consuls in ancient Rome. Fascism began on March 23, 1919, under the leadership of Benito Mussolini. Mussolini was funded primarily by business groups and individuals such as Cornelius Vanderbilt, Thomas Lamont, and many other newspaper and magazine publishers. He was also supported by American bankers.[73]

It is interesting to note that during World War II the three countries with fascist governments were Italy, Germany, and Japan, allies of each other. These same countries are current members of the Group of Seven, which is comprised of the top industrialized countries of the world. Bertram Gross writes:

Although the classic fascists openly subverted constitutional democracy . . . they took great pains to conceal the Big Capital—Big Government partnership. One device for doing this was the myth of "corporatism" or the "corporate state." In place of geographically elected parliaments, the Italians and the Germans set up elaborate systems whereby every interest in the

country—including labor—was to be "functionally represented." In fact, the main function was to provide facades behind
which the decisions were made by intricate networks of business cartels working closely with military officers and their own
people in civilian government.[74]

Does this sound like public private-partnerships? Yes. They use
the same components and systems.

Empowerment of Multinational and Transnational Corporations

In order to understand the power and the philosophy of public-
private partnerships, we need to look at the empowerment of
corporations. The speech by James Gustave Speth at the Rio+5
Conference referred to earlier highlights the "phenomenal growth
of multinational enterprise [a]s a potent force in the global governance."

At one time the corporation that operated in its own country
was called a "national" company. Then as it sought other markets, and started doing business in other countries, it became
"international." As it continued to expand and establish manufacturing facilities and other headquarters overseas, it became
"multinational," and it now had to adhere to the rules and regulations of other countries, do business in other currencies, hire
foreign employees, etc. With the deregulation, or tearing down,
of certain countries' economic restrictions, it became easier for
these countries to conduct business across borders, and the "transnational" corporation (TNC) was birthed. The transnational corporation, because of its great strength, has "transcended" national laws. Additional corporate power has come with extensive
reduction of trade barriers through the General Agreement on
Trade and Tariffs (GATT), now the World Trade Organization
(WTO).

Many multinational and transnational corporations have assets and sales in excess of the value of most small and midsize countries. As if this power were not enough, the Organization for Economic Cooperation and Development (OECD) in Paris is lobbying to pass the Multilateral Agreement on Investments (MAI) which would give corporations unlimited rights in any country that signs the agreement. In the words of Tony Clarke, director of the Polaris Institute in Canada:

> The Multilateral Agreement on Investments is designed to establish a whole new set of global rules for investments that will grant transnational corporations the unrestricted "right" and "freedom" to buy, sell, and move their operations whenever and wherever they want around the world, unfettered by government intervention or regulation. In short, the Multilateral Agreement in Investments seeks to empower transnational corporations . . . by restrict[ing] . . . what national governments can and cannot do.[75]

I think the best definition of fascism, which basically points to everything the Prince of Wales believes and is doing, is: "Fascism adheres to the 'philosopher-king' belief that only one class—which is by birth, education or social standing—is capable of understanding what is best for the whole community and of putting it into practice."[76]

Chapter Eight

The Prince of Wales Business Leaders Forum

The Birth of the Prince of Wales Business Leaders Forum

The structural framework leading up to the current activities of the Prince of Wales Business Leaders Forum is a result of the globalization process that has been ongoing since 1980. Globalization is the breaking down of laws—trade, finance, business, transportation, civil, and commercial—which prohibit across-the-border transactions. In the early 1980s a number of developed countries, including the United States through the passage of the Monetary Control Act of 1980, adopted laws making it legal to invest in other countries. These laws are responsible for more than $1.2 trillion that moves around the world on a daily basis.

The drive for a borderless world economically began in 1944 with the Bretton Woods Monetary Conference. There, seven hundred delegates agreed to establish a World Bank, the International Monetary Fund, and the International Trade Organization. While the Senate ratified the first two organizations, it would not ratify the third. Their reason was to protect our manufacturing base and our trade.

It was not until December 1994 when the Senate passed the General Agreement on Trade and Tariffs (GATT), which became the United Nations World Trade Organization in January 1995 that the final economic foundational stone was laid. In between the passage of the Monetary Control Act and the creation of the WTO was the "fall of communism" and the political change in Russia, which, the Russians say, led to the current "freedoms" through democracy. As a result, the way was opened for a number of *new* actors, such as the corporations, to now work and affect policy on the local level across national borders. The PW-BLF, established in 1990, draws on the prince's vision of sustainable development, the cornerstone for the radical environmental philosophy being pushed on the people of the world.

The Prince of Wales Business Leaders Forum

The 1990 organizational meeting in Charleston was called, "Stakeholders: The Challenge in a Global Market." Over one hundred CEOs from major multinational organizations attended this two-day conference. American firms included Goodyear Tire & Rubber Company, *USA Today,* Sara Lee Corporation, BellSouth, J. C. Penney, Schering-Plough Corporation, Equitable Life, Johnson Publishing, KKR, Monsanto, Pillsbury, the New York Stock Exchange, Exxon, Caterpillar, Procter & Gamble, and Du-Pont. Guests and experts invited to Charleston included United Way of America, King Constantine, Local Initiatives Support Corporation (LISC), Elizabeth Plater-Zyerk (architect of the "holistic" planned community, the Kentlands, in Gaithersburg, Maryland), William Reilly (then administrator with the EPA), Rep. Charles Schumer from the 10th District in New York, Lester Thurow (dean of the Sloan School of Management, Massachusetts Institute of Technology), and Dr. Jessica Tuchman Matthews from the World Resources Institute and member of the CFR.[77] At this conference, the CEOs felt that

> practical experience of business involvement in the community is becoming increasingly important for the career development of business leaders of tomorrow. Education and training

and care for the environment were considered the international priorities.[78]

Some of their conclusions were:

1. CEOs have a critical lead role to play in setting company values and ensuring that local managers are briefed, encouraged, and prepared to listen to local community leaders.
2. Companies must strive to adopt total processes and products based on principles of "sustainable development"—ensuring that use of resources today does not harm the resource needs of future generations.
3. Business executives should assist community leaders in inner cities and isolated rural areas to regenerate their neighborhoods by developing business skills.[79]

It should be noted that this historic organizational conference was held in 1990, two years before the Rio Earth Summit in June 1992, and one year before Charles commended the Brundtland Commission for bringing the term "sustainable development into everyone's vocabulary."

When you think about this meeting and subsequent actions, a "global corporate congress" was held in which a nonprofit charitable organization, the PWBLF, emerged. Why hasn't anyone asked about the authority the prince has assumed? He just roams the globe setting up public-private partnerships with companies, organizations, governments, and institutions from all over the world.

The Business Leaders Forum Directorate

The Prince of Wales Business Leaders Forum is an educational charity with close to fifty multinational corporations from the

United States, Britain, Germany, Japan, and several other countries, on its executive directorate. The U.S. corporations which work very closely with the Prince include 3M, American Express, TRW, Coca-Cola, SmithKline Beecham, ARCO, CIGNA, DHL Worldwide Express, Levi Strauss & Company, the Perot Group, and U.S. WEST International. Additional partners are the American Chamber of Commerce, American Hotel & Motel Association, the Atlanta Project, Charles Stewart Mott Foundation, the City of Charleston, the Ford Foundation, the Kellog Foundation, Eli Lilly, the New York City Housing Partnership, the Office of Ronald Reagan, the Soros Foundation, Texaco, Tufts University, Turner Broadcasting, USAID, and Warnaco.

The Forum is accountable to a board and council made up of the international CEOs and directors from the above listed principal supporters and funded by its members with programs funded by other sponsors, international development agencies and foundations. It works with the World Bank group, United Nations agencies, the European Commission, overseas development agencies, and a number of bilateral agencies from the U.K., Japan, and North America.

The mission of the Prince of Wales Business Leaders Forum is to promote continuous improvement in the practice of good *corporate citizenship* and *sustainable development internationally*, as a natural part of *successful business operations*. It aims to work with members and partners to:

1. Demonstrate that business has an essential and creative role to play in the prosperity of local communities as partners in development, particularly in economies in transition;

2. Raise awareness of the value of corporate responsibility in international business practice;

3. Encourage partnership action between business and communities as an effective means of promoting sustainable economic development.[80]

The PWBLF operates in twenty-six countries, concentrating on post-communist countries and developing economies. They have held twenty-six high-level international meetings in eighteen countries involving five thousand corporate, government, and nongovernmental leaders.

Minnesota Mining and Manufacturing—3M

In America, Minnesota Mining and Manufacturing (3M) is a member of the Prince of Wales Business Leaders Forum. The chairman of the board and chief executive officer of 3M, Livio DeSimone, serves in a number of business, professional, and civic organizations. According to his resume, he is chairman of the World Business Council for Sustainable Development (WBCSD), a member of the U.S./Japan Business Council, a member of the International Advisory Board for the Alliance for Global Sustainability, an ex-officio member of the International Chamber of Commerce Executive Board, and deputy chairman for America on the Prince of Wales Business Leaders Forum, to name some of his affiliations. He has also coauthored a key book on sustainable development entitled *Signals of Change—Business Progress Towards Sustainable Development*, published by the World Business Council for Sustainable Development.

According to their 1996 annual review, the purpose of the World Business Council for Sustainable Development is "to develop closer cooperation between business, government and all other organizations concerned with the environment and sustainable development." They are a coalition of some one hundred twenty international companies from thirty-three countries and twenty major industrial sectors which was formed in January 1995. Mr. DeSimone's letter in the above-referenced annual report states:

It is now almost five years since the Earth Summit in Rio de Janeiro. A paradigm shift clearly has taken place. Business therefore finds itself at the heart of the sustainable development debate. . . . Our mission will be to encourage the business community to act in advance of public opinion or legislation. At all times, the WBCSD's goal will be to ensure that environmental consciousness is placed at the top of business's agenda.

Many of the corporations on the WBCSD are also members of the Prince of Wales Business Leaders Forum. What we can see is a very strong global alliance to ensure that the people of the world adopt the philosophy of sustainable development.

Grand Metropolitan

Let us consider the implications of this concept called sustainable development, which says that we have to be careful we are not depleting the world's resources. What this means is that change is inevitable and that the product cycle, from design and raw materials to manufacturing and distribution, must be re-engineered. Britain's Grand Metropolitan is one of the multinational corporations espousing sustainable development. Grand Metropolitan's Lord Sheppard is vice president/deputy chairman of the Prince of Wales Business Leaders Forum. One of its brochures, entitled *Your Environment . . . We Value It*, explains:

> During the product cycle we also consume natural resources in the form of energy and water. . . . We generate by-products and wastes which require disposal in an environmentally responsible manner. All phases of our business—supply, production, distribution and consumption—face these challenges [waste, polluting the environment, affecting the ozone]. We must all recognize and accept our individual roles, thereby ensuring Grand-Met is a responsible corporate citizen of our planet Earth![81]

In the same brochure GrandMet's chairman, George Bull, writes under the title "Preserving Our Environment for Future Generations":

Recognizing that employees are key to the successful implementation of our environmental actions, GrandMet would like
every employee to look closely at his/her environmental responsibilities. Whether at work or at home, through our involvement in waste reduction, recycling, and other activities, our
environment depends on all of us. Only together can we preserve the environment, invest in our future, and make it a better world for tomorrow![82]

GrandMet also encourages employees to do a number of things
such as "buy items which are better for the environment, use
both sides of the paper, and get involved in community projects
through projects aimed at wildlife preservation, park restoration,
and water conservation."[83]

While I would agree with the "common sense" items like using both sides of the paper, involvement in community projects
aimed at wildlife preservation, park restoration, and water conservation, they are not as wonderful as they sound, but are part
of the quest for control of resources. While it sounds good, one
would have to read UN documents, as I have, to understand what
is behind these concepts. They are not just an "occasional" activity, but part of the end game.

GrandMet, which owns Pillsbury, Burger King, Green Giant,
Hungry Jack, Old El Paso, Jenos, and Progresso, to name a few
of their more well-known nonalcoholic corporations, has a number of public-private partnerships in the United States. "KAPOW"
is one of its projects, in which a "curriculum intervention" was
developed in partnership with the United States National Child
Labor Committee to provide young children with a "window on
the world of work" so children can see the links between school
and a successful adult life. It now operates in twenty U.S. states
through eighty-five partnerships. Over eighty-five hundred children, eight hundred company volunteers, and four hundred educators have participated in the program.[84]

The report issued by the Prince of Wales Business Leaders Forum on all of its activities since 1990 specifies the three types of public-private partnerships used:

1. Partnerships for leveraging resources for specific programs or projects where "programmes and projects" could be either commercial, social or hybrid, where resources are not only financial but also physical, technical, and managerial.
2. Advisory structures to inform, debate, and help to shape the policy agenda.
3. Joint public-private communications campaigns to inform, educate, motivate and mobilize the general public around specific public-interest issues.[85]

Since multinational corporations have profit as their bottom line, the real reason for their interest in partnerships is not necessarily humanitarian. These projects heighten awareness for their product (which is a marketing tool and understandable), enhance their reputation, and help the community they live in. The partnerships are evaluated with regard to whether or not sales volume has increased. For the corporations this is a win-win-win situation:

1. They win with a public-private partnership because they have the money and the power to control.
2. They win with the good works because they can write it off and earn a better reputation.
3. They win because they make money—more money.

Beneath the visual desire to help in the community is money, power, and control. When you combine these three without mercy, justice, or representation, you have a form of government that is different from what is guaranteed in our Constitution.

Activities of the
Prince of Wales Business Leaders Forum

The five-year report (1990–1995) published by the Prince of Wales Business Leaders Forum reveals that it has acted as a catalyst for change on many levels of society, using various conduits such as business, the public sector, nongovernmental organizations, corporations, and international agencies (the World Bank, United Nations, etc.) to foster many different types of partnerships on a global basis. These partnerships all promote a philosophy and world view that is contrary to Genesis 1 and promote Gaia.

The following examples of the activities of the prince's forum are from its book, *Business as Partners in Development.* In 1991 the Japanese Executive Management Training Programme was launched. This is a "unique transnational partnership between the government, business, and nongovernmental sectors." From the business sector there are a number of Japanese and multinational companies that operate in Japan, such as IBM Japan Ltd., ITEC Inc., OMRON Corporation, and Tokyo Electric Power Company, to name a few, as well as a number of young Japanese business leaders. In partnership with the Japanese government and the Prince of Wales Business Leaders Forum, their purpose is to teach corporate citizenship.

Established in 1992, the Central Johannesburg Partnership is a private sector organization committed to involving key stakeholders in central Johannesburg in order to rejuvenate the central city areas. The partnership originally was between businesses, local government, and local community organizations. They have established task forces and focus groups to mobilize business involvement on issues such as transportation, public safety, retail, inner city housing, and urban planning and development. A more recent development is the visioning process for the city.

In 1993 the St. Petersburg initiative was established. Its mission has been discovering how to rejuvenate this historic city, which is also a UNESCO heritage site, and turn it into a tourist attraction. The partnership includes the World Tourism and Travel Academy, American Express, British Air, and Boeing, to name a few, in addition to Grand Metropolitan.

In May 1993, the BOC Group invested in Poland by acquiring a major part of the former Polish state's gas supplier, Polgaz. The new company, BOC Gazy, was formed in partnership with the Polish state treasury and has an active involvement with the Prince of Wales Business Leaders Forum. The idea of a welding school materialized. Since BOC Gazy has major investments in China and has established a cooperative venture with a local university to offer MBA-style training for BOC's Chinese managers, it is a key supporter of the Prince of Wales Business Leaders Forum "Shanghai Business Leadership 2000 Programme."

This venture is in partnership with the PWBLF, the mayor of Shanghai, Shanghai Jiao Tong University, Coopers & Lybrand, and Coca-Cola, to list a few of the corporations. Its purpose is to promote cross-cultural understanding among Chinese and Western business leaders and to help them manage the dramatic economic and social changes they face.

Other partnerships have been created by the Prince of Wales Business Leaders Forum in Hungary, Russia, India, Thailand, India, Vietnam, South Africa, Egypt, Brazil, and Mexico.[86]

Corporate Governance

Although the Prince of Wales Business Leaders Forum was established in 1990, it was not until the president of the World Bank, James Wolfensohn, met the prince in New York in July 1996 that a more formal alliance, we are told, was begun between the two. At the September 1996 annual meeting of the IMF/World Bank, a workshop on corporate governance was conducted. During a telephone interview with James Newsome from the Prince of Wales Business Leaders Forum on September 9, 1997, I was told the PWBLF signed an alliance with the World Bank in early 1997. This alliance is a three-year research project being undertaken by the forum with the bank and the United Nations Development Programme "to identify, analyse, and promote examples of how business is working in partnership with public sector institutions, nongovernmental organizations, and other private sector enterprise, to play a creative and positive role in the process of development."

Stage I was launched at the 1996 IMF/World Bank annual meeting. Stage II will involve "more detailed analysis of the policies and practices of twenty to twenty-five leading multinational companies and industry sectors—reviewing global management structures and key commercial and social activities; assessing their development impacts" in two emerging economies. Stage III was to be completed by the end of 1998 and involves a "survey of stakeholder attitudes to the changing role of business in development." The goals are to "establish new standards and guidelines, stimulate new ideas, provide educational materials and facilitate efforts to replicate or scale-up stakeholder partnerships and examples of good corporate citizenship."[87]

Lastly, it is evident that the prince is orchestrating a major change in world order. All of the above are examples as to how this change will permeate where we live. It is no longer just business, but corporate governance through public-private partnerships. This calls for a complete change in how employees are trained and educated in the company's corporate philosophy, which now becomes the community philosophy. Think about this for a minute. Could the United Nations through "world government" get their policies adopted at the local level? No. However, through corporations the United Nations can change governance and reach each one of us from the CEO, vice president, and mid-level manager, on down to the cleaning crew! If you want to pay your bills, will you quietly agree with the corporate philosophy or will you stand up against it, no matter the cost?

The question to be asked is: Do these CEOs understand what they are doing? I don't know. They might only see the "apple" and not understand the full implications of what they are doing since their participation produces personal monetary rewards and corporate profits. On the other hand, if they are in the prince's "inner circle," then they may know full well. However, once sustainable development is the norm—taught in schools, churches (oh, yes), society, government, and through entertainment—it will replace the values espoused in the Judeo-Christian world view.

It should be noted that in most of the countries around the world, sustainable development has been taught for a number of years. The United States presents the biggest challenge to those who wish to change us. Yet the educational process is already taking place at the University of Michigan, which offers corporate environmental management programs to introduce students to global sustainable development issues in business. At Stanford University's Graduate School of Business, a broad program in corporate citizenship includes elective topics on "Environmental Management" and "Corporate Governance, Power, and Responsibility." The goal is to educate the manager for the twenty-first century as someone who understands the environment, ecology, technology, the social responsibility of the organization—private, public, or nonprofit—and working with NGOs, the public, citizens groups, and public-private partnerships.[88] The reach of the Prince of Wales around the world is deep, vast, and broad, as evidenced in the partners and advisers affiliated with AIESEC, which include (in addition to the Prince of Wales Business Leaders Forum) the Club of Rome, the Society for International Development (former UN secretary-general Boutros-Boutros-Ghali is now president), and the United Nations Development Programme (James Speth), and UNESCO.[89] These, along with all of the other partners mentioned in this article, reveal a man with immense power.

Chapter Nine

The Real Charles

Charles—The Hidden Prince (see Appendix C)

In an interview that Prince Charles gave on BBC's "Newsnight" program in 1994, he expressed his devotion to his work for Britain and the Commonwealth. He said, "So much I try to do is behind the scenes. So it is difficult for people to understand how all the things fit together." He also asserted that there is a common theme to all his projects and insisted they will turn out to be for the long term good.[90]

This is correct. The real work of Charles is not being covered or reported by the mainstream world press. In addition, those who participate with the prince do not make it visible, either. For example, the president of Coca-Cola recently died. In the obituary of Robert C. Goizueta, it never mentioned his work with the PWBLF. You would think that this would be one of the highlights of his career.

Unlike the Grand Metropolitan and 3M corporations, Coca-Cola's 1996 annual report, while it highlighted its vast international endeavors, only spent a line or two on the environment, and did not even mention their substantial involvement with the PWBLF.

The 1995 and 1996 annual reports of ITOCHU, while more friendly and informative in their presentation, highlighted the environment and global memberships, but did not mention the Prince of Wales Business Leaders Forum. The same is true for

BMW's 1996 annual report. I found, in looking at a number of the annual reports for the PWBLF principal supporters and advisors, that only the ones mentioned above reference the forum. You would think this would be something they all would shout from the roof tops, after all they are "hobnobbing" with royalty!

When I attended Rio+5 in March 1997 in Rio de Janeiro, I asked the executive director of the International Chamber of Commerce, Maria Cattaui, who their counterparts were on the global level and if they were effecting the same thing. I then mentioned the Prince of Wales Business Leaders Forum. It was a like-minded colleague of mine, Joan Peros, who pointed out to me later that my question took Miss Cattaui by surprise and made one of the other members of the panel turn deep red (Bjorn Stigson from the World Business Council for Sustainable Development). Miss Cattaui did speak about the ICC's activities, but never addressed the question of the Prince of Wales Business Leaders Forum.

Not deterred, I questioned the president of the World Bank, James Wolfensohn, during his press briefing at the same conference. He, too, digressed, and eventually got around to the prince. He said:

> In the case of Prince Charles [and the PWBLF], it's a very interesting organization in two particular respects. He's doing what I think is very important work . . . to get British industry conscious and working with him on issues of social responsibility and on the environment. H[is] group of British industrialists . . . share the sort of values we espouse here. We are working with him . . . not because he is the Prince of Wales, but because it is a very good program. The second thing he has done is to have a program for youth, which is a remarkable program. I was interested because he seems to know how to do it quite well in English-speaking countries.

Lastly, the Templeton Award for Progress in Religion is an interesting example of Charles's hidden work. Funded by Sir John Templeton, an American from humble beginnings who won a scholarship to Yale, was chosen as a Rhodes Scholar, and was knighted by the queen in 1987. Since the award's inception in 1972, there have been twenty-six recipients from all over the world and from all of the world's religions—Christianity, Buddhism, Hinduism, Islam, etc. According to Donald Lehr, with whom I spoke on October 21, 1997, the Templeton Award for Progress in Religion is "an interfaith, international award."[91] This appears to fit in quite well with the goal and objective of the United World Colleges and Charles desire to be "defender of faith."

It is interesting to note that the recipients have to go to Buckingham Palace to receive the monetary portion of the award and to meet with Prince Philip. When I pressed about why they had to go to the palace (after all, it is given by an individual, not the royal family), I was told the award is given in British pounds (which does not make a lot of sense). Mr. Lehr told me that the 1998 award will be given at the United Nations headquarters instead of Buckingham Palace.

Some of the recipients from the catholic and non-catholic faiths have been Mother Teresa, Dr. Billy Graham, Charles Colson, and Dr. Bill Bright. The judges include people from all walks and faiths. Judges from business include the CEOs of C. Itoh, Gallup, W. R. Grace and Company, N. M. Rothschild & Sons, to name a few. United States presidents and senators include Presidents Ford and Bush, Senators Danforth, Hatch, and Hatfield. Religious leaders include Dr. Eugene Carson Blake, past general secretary of the World Council of Churches, USA; Lord Coggan, past Archbishop of Canterbury; the Dalai Lama; Dr. Inamullah Khan, past secretary-general of the World Muslim Congress; Rev. David Mainse, president of Crossroads Christian Communications; Dr. Norman Vincent Peale, past minister at Marble Collegiate Church; and Sir Robin Woods, who was Bishop of Worcester and chaplain to Queen Elizabeth II. Members of royalty in-

Is this the real Prince Charles?

clude Prince Albert of Belgium, Queen Fabiola of Belgium, Dr. Otto Von Habsburg (the Habsburg dynasty), Grand Duchess Josephine of Luxembourg, and Prince Charles.[92]

Prince Charles, the Inn Keeper

In 1992 the Prince of Wales Business Leaders Forum was approached by the chief executive of the Inter-Continental Hotels and Resorts with a new idea to utilize the environmental experience of the forum in developing an industry-wide environmental initiative. A group of international hotels signed a compact, and the International Hotel Environment Initiative (IHEI) was born. IHEI consists of a network of hoteliers working through a dedicated support unit with the goal to *change business behavior* across the entire hotel industry. Industry leaders will improve the environmental performance in their own hotels and act as examples for others. In the five years since the initiative was started, IHEI has produced a number of materials, such as the *Green Hotelier*, an environmental action packet for hotels produced in partnership with the International Hotel Association, the United Nations Environment Programme (UNEP), and various hotel associations, such as the American Hotel and Motel Association, the Caribbean Hotel Association, Thailand Hotel Association, and the Hotel Association of Hungary.

One of their environmental initiatives is the Linens and Towels Rescue Program which encourages hotel guests to conserve on daily linen replacement and help hotels save on water and detergent. The Holiday Inn Worldwide began its "Conserving for Tomorrow" program in 1994, stating: "The Holiday Inn Worldwide will pro-actively encourage and pursue initiatives to improve the global environment."[93]

While I do not disagree with the concept of how often a guest wishes to change linens, for whatever reason, it masks the true philosophy of sustainable development, which is control of all resources on planet Earth. People are being conditioned and it is coming from the global to the local level through business.

Hotels in partnership with the Prince of Wales Business Leaders Forum include the biggest, most luxurious in the world, such as ACCOR, Forte, Hilton International, Holiday Inn Worldwide, ITT Sheraton, Inter-Continental, Mandarin Oriental Hotel Group, Marriott Lodging Group, Marco Polo Hotels, Radisson SAS Hotels Worldwide, Renaissance Hotels International, and the Taj Group of Hotels.[94] Look for their special signs inviting you to keep your towels and linens for more than one day to help them save money!

Prince Charles—The Defender of Faith
As a result of my personal study and in light of the above, I have

come to believe that when the United States ratified the United Nations Charter, we and the other countries of the world who were not part of Britain's Commonwealth, reverted back under British rule through the United Nations organizational structure. Therefore the fulfillment of the Rhodes Trust is complete.

If the Rhodes legacy is now complete through the UN, then what we are seeing besides world government and the accompanying economic infrastructure, which is environmentally sustainable, is also a world religion. Charles negates the resurrection of Jesus Christ, reducing him to a "good teacher" or "prophet," along with Mohammed, Confucius, and the other founders of the world's religions. Charles is pagan in his religious beliefs, worshipping the earth—creation—instead of the Creator. The UN's infatuation with paganism can be seen not only in Gaia worship, but with the Indian tribal chiefs that parade around at many of their conferences. Once the opening tribal dance is performed, these pathetic individuals are then used for photo opportunities.

The movement toward a world religion can be seen in the establishment of a United Religions Organization. At the United Nations fiftieth anniversary in San Francisco in June 1995, I interviewed the Right Reverend William E. Swing, bishop of California and trustee of Grace Cathedral, who is one of the founders of the newly established United Religions Organizations. Grace Cathedral is where the founders of the UN held a service commemorating their efforts to finalize the United Nations Charter in 1945. Since Bishop Swing is the key motivator behind what could be called the "United Nations of World Religions," I asked him what part Grace Cathedral played at the time. He answered:

Well, fifty years ago there was a service at Grace Cathedral for the United Nations and in those days, I must say, it didn't look anything like today's service [referring to the service which Princess Margaret attended]. In those days you would just come to a Christian cathedral and you'd have a Christian service and that was on behalf of the whole world and that was the way it was done. Fifty years later, the world has changed dramatically and we've had to broaden our understanding of God [so] that we have to not only tolerate, not only respect, but we have to move beyond that [understanding] to enter into the higher pursuit of a relationship with God, with people from all the religions of the world. The world is getting smaller and smaller. There's one financial world. There's more or less one newspaper world. There's one entertainment world. But there's one aspect of the world that has not developed and that is, there's not a soul of the world. There's no place where the great striving and the spiritual yearnings of the world can be expressed and the conscious of the world can be voiced in one place. So that's where we're aiming.

He continued: "Instead of having our own tribal religious identities, that we can now begin to think in terms of broadening the religious dialogue . . . so that we can make it as a community."

In other words, if you disagree with the world ecumenical religious movement that is being propagated, you are not keeping peace in the community. The United Religions Organization and the holistic beliefs of Prince Charles are setting the stage for one of his future titles, "Defender of Faith" (see Appendix D).

King Charles III

There has been much speculation with regard as to when Charles will become king. I surmise that he does not need a throne, for he already has one. The environmental agenda via sustainable development, and public-private partnerships with the world's largest and strongest multinational corporations, many of which have cash flows and assets exceeding that of most countries, provide Charles his throne. It appears that he rules behind the scenes, encouraging, expanding, and pushing the agenda of the United Nations, partnering with the World Bank and other global agencies, all of which are advancing world government, a philosophy with which he is not uncomfortable. After all, there have been many kings, popes, and world leaders who have tried to attain it.

When one takes a look at the forty-eight companies on the prince's directorate, twenty-three of them are part of *Business Week's* "Global 1,000" corporations, with a combined market value of over $1 trillion. Apart from the manufacturing base he has amassed, travel and tourism is the world's largest industry and generator of jobs. It provides direct and indirect employment for two hundred million people, one in every nine workers in the world. Its gross domestic product generates more than that of the gross national product (GNP) of the United States in 1995.

It is through public-private partnerships that corporations will replace a nation's governance. It appears with Charles at the head of the PWBLF that corporations will take their lead from him. When you have a partnership's board of appointed people representing government, corporations, the private sector, and nongovernmental organizations, *money* rules, not government or the people. What we see in the making is a new form of governance *transcending national borders*, elected officials, and the will of the people. Little by little, people will be squeezed out and the New World Order will fully emerge.

The environment is something all the people of the world share—the air, water, fish, and fowl. Whoever controls the environment, controls man. That is the objective and goal. The work that Prince Charles is spearheading has been gaining momentum. He is at the heart of what is going on in the world as it relates to power, control, philosophy, and "forward" thinking at every level of society.

Since Prince Charles lives and breathes sustainable development, a better title for him would be the "Sustainable Prince."

Conclusion

Because of who he is, doors automatically open and people flock to him. His tentacles are very long, reaching into every area of life, business, and government. He transcends politics, national borders, and religion. He is very powerful by way of position, lineage, inheritance, importance, and influence. He is out to remake society and mold it into his image, which is based on Gaia and corporate global governance through public-private partnerships. This will change life for every person on earth as we will become slaves to the new twenty-first century feudal landlords—those with the power and money. Sustainable development demands that every crust of bread eaten be measured against what a person produces in order to protect resources for future generations. Is all of this the new divine right of kings? Do you not realize the second American Revolution is in the process of being fought? The battle this time is philosophical, no guns or bullets. It is spiritual warfare at its finest. The person the mainstream media would have us believe Charles is—is not the real Charles. The real Charles has a global agenda of his own. He should be recognized as a *very major player* in the end-time game. What is your response?

Appendix A

People's Millennium Assembly

In September 2000, exactly fifty-five years after its founding, the United Nations will add representative government to its structure so the people of the world can have a "say in their deliberations." This will provide them with legitimacy as the people of the world bypass their national governments and go directly to the international level with their problems. To those of us who know truth, understanding that the United Nations is a world government is not new. By adding a "People's Parliament" or a "People's Millennium Assembly" to its structure suggests that they feel they are so far along in the process that there will not be any opposition to their actions. As you will read in a later appendix, Prince Charles is also working toward adding representative government to the UN, as one of his organizations is a co-convener of the Gorbachev State of the World Forum. The one-worlders are also working on a global tax and to add a rapid deployment force. Unfortunately, many of these globalists are in the U.S. House and Senate, as House Bill 4453 was introduced in June 2000 to provide the UN with a rapid deployment force—your sons and grandsons may serve in it. This suggestion has been made over and over again in the last century and has finally made its appearance in the House.

Before we get into the nuts and bolts of the People's Millennium Assembly, which was discussed in chapter six, let us take a look at the history which has brought us to this point.

Background History

While *Prince Charles: The Sustainable Prince* has dealt with Cecil Rhodes and his dream to bring America back under British rule, it was the British who began clamoring for a world organization through major speeches and a pamphlet called *The League of Nations, a Practical Suggestion,* released in December 1918. In discussing the idea, the Milner Group published an article written by one of its very important members, Lionel Curtis. In it, he wrote: "The League must not be a world government. If the burden of a world government is placed on it, it will fall with a crash." He pointed out it could be a world government only if it represented peoples and not states, and if it had the power to tax those peoples.

As you know, our Senate very wisely in the 1920s refused to ratify the League of Nations Treaty. The League went away by itself to Switzerland, where it continued to set up its structure until the time when the world would be ready for it. That time came in 1945 after a second world war when its successor, the United Nations, which was heartily endorsed by President Roosevelt (who named the new global structure), claimed to be a place where the world leaders could come together to discuss their differences to avert war. We should point out that FDR made more than eight hundred speeches in support of the League of Nations.

In the fifty-five years since its founding, a government structure has evolved rather than a conference type of arrangement, suggesting something more powerful and more deliberate. If you were to take a look at the cabinet level departments of our government, you would find for each department that there is a corresponding agency or committee at the United Nations. For example, the Office of President corresponds to that of the Secretary General; the Department of Defense to the Security Council; the Department of Treasury to the International Monetary Fund/World Bank; the Department of State to the General Assembly; the Department of Trade to the World Trade Organization; the Department of Labor to the International Labor Organization (ILO); the Department of Education to the United Nations Educational, Scientific and Cultural Organization (UNESCO); the Department of Health and Human Services to the World Health Organization (WHO) and UNICEF; the Department of Agriculture to the United Nations Food and Agriculture Organization (FAO); the Department of the Interior to the United Nations Development Programme (UNDP) and the United Nations Environmental Programme (UNEP); and the Supreme Court to the World Court. Lastly, it appears that the Justice Department will correspond to the recently established International Criminal Court. The only thing it appears to lack is a chamber for representatives by the people of the world, taxation, and its own army, all of which are currently in the process of coming together.

In May 2000, a preparatory conference was held in New York at the United Nations. I had the privilege to attend and to obtain a number of interviews.

People's Millennium Assembly

Activists

The people who gave the world the International Criminal Court and the Land Mine Treaty, have come together once again to give us a "People's Parliament." Officers of the Millennium Forum, which is the umbrella organization, include co-chairs from Bahai International and the UN, with vice-chairs divided up by regions. Europe is represented by a World Federation of United Nations Associations, the International Youth and Student Movement for the UN. North America is represented by the World Federalist Movement. Other groups and organizations which are forum associates and contributors include: Child Welfare League, International Council of Jewish Women, International Federation of Social Workers, International Union for Land Value Taxation,

Lawyers' Committee on Nuclear Policy, Lucius Trust, Pathways to Peace, Queens Chinese Women's Association, Sisters of Mercy, and ZONTA International, to name a few. Contributing individuals include: Sylvan Barnet from Rotary International, Dianne Dillon-Ridgley from Worldwide YWCAs, Alan Kay and Hazel Henderson (friends of Gorbachev and outright Marxists), Robert Kauffman Building Services from the Association of World Citizens, and Norma Levitt, NGO representative, World Union for Progressive Judaism.

Background

In the July 1997 set of proposals for United Nations reform, Secretary-General Kofi Annan called for the designation of the year 2000 session of the General Assembly as "a Millennium Assembly," which he said should "focus on preparing the United Nations to meet the major challenges and needs of the world community in the twenty-first century." He said, it should be accompanied by a "People's Assembly."

People and Ideas

Two of the numerous interviews which I did stand out: The first was Dr. Andrew Strauss, associate professor of international law at Widener University School of Law, who along with Dr. Richard Falk, are the leaders in the idea of an electoral assembly on the global level to represent you and I. The second was Titus Alexander.

Dr. Andrew Strauss

Dr. Strauss delivered an important speech with regard to the broad framework. He said:

> I think if this meeting is about anything, we could think of [it] symbolically where civil society [NGOs] has been officially called in to have this meeting at the UN as the end of the "Old Para-

digm." And what is the *Old Paradigm of sovereignty?* [emphasis added]. It says, citizens, if they are going to be represented at the international level, are going to be represented through their states. The International Order—is between nations and states and it is the interstate order. The only role for civil society is within their states so the best you can have as a citizen's group is to lobby your own government and have them represent your interest at the international level. I think that the old idea of sovereignty of politics for citizens within or between states is over.

He went on to give a number of proposals for how this new international arrangement would work. Basically he supports the idea of a directly elected assembly by all the people of the world which would create some sort of advisory body with lawmaking powers over time. Using the model of elected representatives in the United States as his model, he said that the elections would help the process be noticed.

It would have great legitimacy and put the opponents of it and those who didn't like it in the position to either give it legitimacy or they would have to go into the fray and fight with us and in the process of doing so, would legitimize it more and more—much the same way it did in England when they first started a Parliament, which was at first only advisory to the king.

This is what has been put into the final document to be presented to the General Assembly.

In an interview with him, I asked about the problem with public-private partnerships which is a partnership between governments, corporations, and NGOs (civil society).

Veon: With regard to the strengthening of civil society, civil society is greatly strengthened through public-private partnerships. Could you address this with regard to various comments you made on different ways for civil society to become more empowered?

Strauss: We are in a bit of a hybrid situation which doesn't fit any models of political theory right now—the way that civil society and states are coming together. I think it is the most effective strategy for states and civil society together to push for progressive initiatives which they both support because that is what made the Land Mines Treaty successful, the International Criminal Court and the Global Warming Treaty, as well. All three are examples in which civil society got together with governments.

Veon: How do you see the role of the NGOs and corporate society, as many NGOs are being funded by the corporations? How are safeguards going to be put in place between those relationships?

Strauss: Obviously it's a very, very trick question, and there are tremendous possibilities for co-option. It is one of the reasons why I support some sort of electoral assembly, because I ultimately believe that civil society organizations, to claim the voice of the people rather than lobbyists groups, is very problematic, even if they aren't infiltrated by corporate money. The accusation can be easily made, "Just who do they represent, other than themselves?" So we need some sort of system which rests on some sort of popular legitimacy through some sort of representative electoral model and have civil society organizations championing their causes.

Titus Alexander—Charter99

Titus Alexander is with the Charter99 group, which is sponsored through the United Nations Association of Great Britain. The charter is a very interesting document and can be found at *www.charter99.org*. It credits new energy and precision for international government: "The Commission on Global Governance and their efforts to draw up a framework for global politics—the Hague Agenda for Peace, Jubilee 2000, the campaigning to create an International Criminal Court."

Charter99 goes on to say:

> It is that in many ways we now have world government. It is not to be found at the United Nations. Rather the UN has been sidelined, while the real business of world government is done elsewhere. Global policies are discussed and decided behind closed doors by exclusive groups such as the G8, OECD, the Bank for International Settlements, the World Bank, the International Monetary Fund, the World Trade Organization, and others. Together they have created what can be seen as dominant and exclusive institutions of world government. All too often they are influenced by transnational corporations which pursue their own world strategies.

The purpose of Charter99 is to "start the new century by initiating the process of democratic global governance based on openness and accountability." The key word is "accountability." This new document calls for accountability to all the above groups. What makes this effort so interesting is that Titus Alexander tells me he wrote to scores of people and organizations to get their endorsement. Some of those who endorse his effort include: Jonathan Dimbleby, authored most of Prince Charles official biographies; Jonathan Porrit, a very good friend of Prince Charles; Sir Shridath Ramphal, co-chairman of the Commission on Global Governance, who Alexander said called him up on a Sunday after to congratulate him on this document (Sir Ramphal also served as the president of the Commonwealth for over ten years and worked very closely with the queen. How very common!); Anita Roddick, president of BodyWorks and closely affiliated with Prince Charles; and about two dozen with titles of Baroness, Lord, and Sir. When I asked him if the Prince of Wales Business Leaders Forum had endorsed Charter99, he told me he had not written to them yet. I find this and the fact that the number of individuals who have close ties with the queen or the Prince of Wales very interesting. I don't think it is coincidental!

Charter99 supports twelve areas for urgent action, which include: monitor and regulate international corporations and financial institutions; strengthen the UN peacekeeping and multilateral global security; create equal world citizenship based on the UN Declaration of Human Rights and covenants; ratify the International Criminal Court; create an International Environmental Court; and make poverty reduction a global priority.

The People's Millennium Forum Declaration and Agenda for Action

The preparatory document which they worked on and which will be presented to the General Assembly in September represents the work of thirteen hundred fifty representatives of over one thousand NGOs and other civil society organizations. This in a world of hardly eight billion represents the people of the world! However, this document is twenty-one pages long. They provide a "Vision Statement" and then enumerate numerous duties for governments and civil society. As you read through, you will see that it is a far cry from our Constitution and Bill of Rights.

Vision

Our vision is of a world that is human-centered and genuinely democratic. In our vision, we are one human family, in all our diversity, living on one common homeland and sharing a just, sustainable, and peaceful world, guided by universal principles of democracy, equality, inclusion, volunteerism, nondiscrimination, and participation by all persons, men and women, young and old, regardless of race, faith, disability, sexual orientation, ethnicity, or nationality. It is a world where peace and human security, as envisioned in the principles of the United Nations Charter, replace armaments, violent conflicts, and wars.

Eradication of Poverty, Including Social Development and Debt Cancellation

1. The UN: To act as an independent arbitrator to balance the interest of debtor and creditor nations and to monitor how debt cancellation funds are spent.
2. To immediately establish at the UN a Global Poverty Eradication Fund, which will ensure that poor people have access to credit, with contributions from governments, corporations, and the World Bank and other sources.
3. *To cancel debts of developing countries, including odious debts, the repayment of which diverts funds from basic needs.*
4. Civil Society: To develop new relations and partnerships among community institutions, educators, scientists, researchers, local authorities, business, labor, and NGOs.
5. Civil Society: To exert our best efforts to implement the Universal Declaration of Human Rights.

Peace, Security, and Disarmament

The UN and its member states have failed to fulfill their primary responsibility of maintaining peace. The Forum urges:

1. The UN: To carry out the objective of moving toward the abolition of war, the UN should develop a draft proposal for global disarmament to be discussed at a special session on Disarmament.
2. To assist the Security Council on conflict prevention in a more flexible way, the General Assembly should establish an open-ended Conflict Prevention Committee to serve a rapid action conflict prevention and early warning function.
3. *To expand the UN Arms register to show production and sale of small arms and light weapons.*
4. *To establish ready police and peacekeeping forces.*

Facing the Challenge of Globalization: Equity, Justice, and Diversity

1. UN: To reform and democratize all levels of decision making

in the Bretton Woods institutions and TWO and integrate them fully into the United Nations system, making these institutions ACCOUNTABLE to the Economic and Social Council [ECOSOC, one of the UN organs].

2. To move toward democratic political control of the global economy so that it may serve our vision.

3. Governments: To make serious commitments to restructure the global financial architecture based on principles of equity, transparency, accountability, and democracy, and to balance, with the participation of civil society organizations, the monetary means to favor human endeavor, and ecology such as an alternative time-based currency. *To give particular attention to eradication of unequal taxation and to impose new forms of taxation such as the Tobin tax, and regional and national capital controls.*

Human Rights

The United Nations human rights treaty regime, composed of the Universal Declaration of Human Rights, the Covenants and Conventions, is acknowledged to be one of the three core objectives of the United Nations–Human Rights, Development, and Peace.

1. The indivisibility, interdependence, and interrelatedness of all human rights have been repeatedly reaffirmed at the level of rhetoric. However, the practice civil and political rights have been given a higher priority than economic, social, and cultural rights, often to the detriment of both sets of rights.

2. The Forum urges the United Nations to strengthen the existing international human rights system to ensure full recognition, respect for, and realization of human rights for all; and implement all those UN resolutions calling for self-determination and an end to military occupation. To protect the rights of people under military occupation. To establish a fair and effective International Criminal Court.

Sustainable Development and the Environment

Sustainable development is the recognition that environment and development issues should be addressed in an integrated manner.

1. The Forum urges the United Nations to strengthen its capacity to monitor governments and require their compliance with Agenda 21, their commitments to Rio, commitments made during the Commission on Sustainable Development meetings, the Copenhagen Declaration, and the Convention on Biological Diversity and the Convention on Climate Change.

2. To encourage its organs, especially UNEP and UNDP, to actively support the establishment of sustainability centres to advise local governments on the *implementation of Agenda 21 in local communities through comprehensive, integrated development policies and strategies.*

3. To endorse the *Earth Charter in the UN General Assembly.*

Strengthening and Democratizing the United Nations and International Organizations

A major task of the world community in the twenty-first century will be to strengthen and greatly enhance the role of the United Nations in the global context. Governments must recommit themselves to the realization of the goals and mandates of the United Nations Charter.

1. The Forum urges the United Nations to strengthen the coordinating role of the UN General Assembly to ensure that it can fulfill the mandates it already has according to the UN Charter.

2. To make sure the Security Council is more representative of the world.

3. To limit and move toward eliminating the use of the veto.

4. To develop a more effective means not requiring the use of force to prevent the outbreak of war.

5. To make the International Court of Justice the locus of a more effective, integrated system of international justice.

6. *To consider the creation of a UN parliamentary body related to the UN General Assembly. Our proposal is the creation of a consultative Parliamentary Assembly which should have its membership elected through an election process.*

7. *To move toward the creation of alternative revenue sources for the United Nations. The UN should set up expert groups and begin the necessary intergovernmental negotiations toward establishing alternative revenue resources, which could include fees for the commercial use of the oceans, fees for airplane use of the skies, fees for use of the electromagnetic spectrum, fees on the foreign exchange transactions (Tobin Tax), and a tax on the carbon content of fuels.*

8. *Civil Society: To support the creation and funding of a Global Civil Society Forum to meet at least every two to three years and that such a forum is conducted democratically and transparently and is truly representative of all sectors of civil society and all parts of the world.*

Appendix B

The Prince of Wales Business Leaders Forum

HRH, Prince of Wales, President
Robert Davies, Chief Executive

Vice-President/Deputy Chairman
3M—Livio DeSimone*
Grand Metropolitan—Lord Sheppard*
British Petroleum—Sir D. Simon*
Wheelock & Co.—Peter Woo*
Cable & Wireless—Rt. Hon. Lord Young*

Vice-President/Board Members
ABB Asea Brown Boveri—Percy Barnevik*
Johnson Matthey—D. Davies*
TRW, Inc.—J. Gorman*
Coca-Cola- Neville Isdell*
SmithKline Beecham—J. Leschley*
ITOCHU—M. Murofushi
BMW AG—B. Pischetsrieder*

Advisory Members
ARCO—Lod Cook
Volkswagen—Dr. C. Hahn
Top Technology—H. Fitzgibbons

London First—S. O'Brien*
Young & Rubicam—L. Snoddon*
Grand Metropolitan—D. Nash—Hon. Treasurer

Advisors

Burson-Marsteller
Dentsu Burson-Marsteller
Environmental Resources Management Ltd.
Jonathon Porritt
Members of **International Partnership Network**
Takeo Shiina (IBM Japan)
Clarke Whitehill
Bates, Wells & Braithwaite
Two other individuals

Principal Supporters

ABB Asea Brown Boveri Ltd, (Switzerland)
BMW AG (Germany)
British Petroleum (BP) (UK)
Cable and Wireless (UK)
Coca-Cola Company (US)
Grand Metropolitan (UK)
ITOCHU Corp. (Japan)
Johnson Matthey (UK)
3M (US)
SmithKline Beecham (UK/US)
TRW (US)
Wheelock & Co. Ltd., (Hong Kong)

Council Members

Abercrombie & Kent Group (UK/US)
ALKAN Group (Egypt)
Allianz AG (Germany)
AMERICAN EXPRESS Bank Ltd. (US)
ARCO (US)

ARTOC Group (Egypt)

Bajaj Auto Ltd. (India)

British Gas (UK)

BSO Beheer BV/Origin (Netherlands)

CIGNA Corp. (US)

Coopers & Lybrand (UK)

D'elegant Holding Ltd. (Hong Kong)

DHL Wordwide Express, S.A. (US)

The Fuji Bank Inc. (Japan)

Kolon Group (Korea)

KPMG (UK)

Levi Strauss & Co. (US)

Lorentzen Empreendimentos, S.A. (Brazil)

McKinsey & Company, Inc. (UK)

Norsk Hydro a.s. (Norway)

Obayashi Corp. (Japan)

Pasona Inc. (Japan)

The Perot Group (US)

Robert Bosch GmbH (Germany)

Sami Saad & Co. (Egypt)

Sedgwick Group (UK)

The Sumitomo Bank, Ltd. (Japan)

Tata Industries Ltd. (India)

Tokyo Electric Power Co. (Japan)

Tokyo Motor Corp. (Japan)

U.S. WEST International (US)

Note: American companies are boldfaced. Corporations which are part of *Business Week* "Global 1000" corporations are italicized. (*Directors)

Additional Partners, Members, Funders, and Associates
PWBLF in Partnership with IHEI

United States
American Chamber of Commerce, Egypt

American Hotel & Motel Assoc.
American Express Bank Ltd.
American Express TRS
American Express Travel/Tourism
American Chamber of Commerce
Associated Press
Association for Community Development
Association of Industry & Land Protection
Association of Progressive Communications
The Atlanta Project
Charles Stewart Mott Foundation
City of Charleston
Ford Foundation
Friends of the Earth
Hilton International
Kellogg Foundation
New York City Housing Partnership
Office of Ronald Reagan
Soros Foundations
Texaco, Inc.
Tufts University
Turner Broadcasting Corp.
USAID and Warnaco Inc.

Other

Aga Khan Foundation
Air Canada
Du Pont Australia
European Bank for Reconstruction and Development
   (EBRD—World Bank)
Inter-American Development Bank (IADB)—World Bank
Shanghai Jiao Tong University
Shell China
Slovak Union of Nature and Landscape Protectors

Slovak Academic Information Agency
St. Petersburg Legislative Assembly
St. Petersburg Institute of Cultural Programmers
St. Petersburg Institute of Medical & Social Problems
    & Management
St. Petersburg Institute Women & Mgmt.
St. Petersburg Mayor's Office
St. Petersburg Partnership Initiative Business Supporters Group
St. Petersburg Press
St. Petersburg Renaissance Foundation
St. Petersburg State University
United Nations Development Programme
United Nations Environment Programme
World Bank Group
World Economic Forum

**The International Hotel Environmental Initiative—
    IHEI**

International Council
Accor Hotels
Forte Hotels
Hilton International
Holiday Inn Worldwide
ITT Sheraton
Inter-Continental Hotels Group
Mandarin Oriental Hotel Group
Marriott Lodging Group
Marco Polo Hotels & Resorts
Radisson SAS Hotels Worldwide
Renaissance Hotels International
The Taj Group of Hotels

Compiled by: The Women's International Media Group, Inc. 301/570-
7525.

SOURCE: Prince of Wales Business Leaders Forum 1990–1995 Report.

The Coming Out
of the Prince of Wales

Ever since I wrote *Prince Charles: The Sustainable Prince,* I have been watching his gradual "coming out." For those not attuned to the prince's real job, they would not be looking in the first place. Since the prince is quite sophisticated and only deals with those who are rich and powerful—world leaders, other related royalty, and CEOs from the world's biggest multinational and transnational corporations—they would not look in business magazines and newspapers.

Financial Times on "Responsible Business"

The first major coming out was a series of articles in *Financial Times,* which were sponsored by the Prince of Wales Business Leaders Forum (PWBLF) in the spring/summer of 1999. An inserted magazine entitled "Responsible Business" basically discussed partnerships, corporate responsibility, globalization, how the Prince of Wales Business Leaders Forum looks at the building of "shareholder value-added and societal value-added" aspects. In a foreword by Mark Moody-Stuart, chairman of the Committee of Managing Directors Royal Dutch/Shell Group of Companies, he said:

> On the even of the twenty-first century, the great challenge facing our society is how to build a *sustainable future.* We there-

fore wholeheartedly support the work of the Prince of Wales Business Leaders Forum in contributing *throughout the world* to the development of responsible business practice. Working together in this way to incorporate this thinking into every company's activity will deliver the legacy of a sustainable future for the generations still to come.

(emphasis added)

Needless to say, the magazine is filled with the public-private partnership arrangements, using sustainable development as its philosophical basis. In the article, "ethics without frontiers," it says:

A "partnership revolution" is taking place across the globe, according to the Prince of Wales Business Leaders Forum. It claims its recent surveys of companies' activities have revealed an array of new partnerships—"dazzling in terms of their variety and scope"—which are helping to promote ethical relationships with communities around the world and achieve traditional core business goals. Business in the Community [which the prince helped found]—which over the past decade has swelled in size to include three-quarters of the FTSE 100 as members—is an example of such work in the UK, and there are similar bodies around the world.

The PWBLF is at the *core* of developing new strategies and rules with regard to how corporations will work with communities to build sharehold value-added and societal value-added benefits. It would take another book to explain these new and complex relationships which are in the process of replacing the relationships we have known where corporations have no business in government or in managing communities. Basically what we are seeing is if corporations are partnering with governments and "sharing" the responsibilities that governments use to perform, what the PWBLF is doing is creating a "global business constitution" called corporate governance—which includes corporate ethics, which will replace the "old paradigm" of government. For further information on the PWBLF, log on to his website at *www.pwblf.org.*

The Gorbachev State of the World Forum

While it is true Russia used to be ruled by relatives of the prince which were displaced by the communists, Prince Charles has buried the sickle and is helping to convene the sixth annual Gorbachev State of the World Forum 2000. The forum, which is being moved from San Francisco to New York City to help highlight the "People's Millennium Assembly," has numerous sponsors which include: the Progressio Foundation in partnership with the Prince of Wales Trust, the World Business Council on Sustainable Development, the U.K. Industrial Society, PriceWaterhouseCoopers, and the European Business Network for Social Cohesion. The theme is, "Shaping Globalization: Convening the Community of Stakeholders." Their press invitation states:

> Working with partners worldwide, the Forum will convene a high-level gathering of international leaders timed to coincide with the historic United Nations Millennium Summit in New York. The intent of the Forum and its partners in juxtaposing Forum 2000 with the UN Millennium Summit is to convene a "global town hall meeting" to bring the major stakeholders together in a process of mutual deliberation.
>
> The Forum is working with the following partners:
>
> 1. **Heads of State**. The Forum is negotiating with several dozen nations concerning their participation.
> 2. **Emerging leaders** from Africa, Latin America, East Asia, India, and the Middle East.
> 3. **Business Sector**. Working with the Progressio Foundation,

and other co-conveners, the theme for business is "Making a Profit While Making a Difference."

4. **Trade Unions**. In partnership with the AFL-CIO, the United Steelworkers of America, and the Textile Workers, among others, to bring leaders of trade unions from around the world. Juan Somavia, director general of the International Labor Organization, will moderate a dialogue.

5. **Civil Society Organizations**. This includes The Synergos Institute, the Global South, the World Wildlife Fund, the Earth Council, the International Forum on Globalization, among others.

6. **Science and Technology Sector**. In partnership with a group of Silicon Valley executives, the International Space Sciences Organization, and the John Templeton Foundation to convene a spectrum of specialists in the sciences, physics, and high technology to participate in the dialogues on globalization.

The intent is to work with partners worldwide to accomplish two objectives: to help galvanize the emergence of the private sector and civil society as key players in global governance; and to keep the questions of ethics and equity on the forefront of humanity's decisions related to globalization and the applications of scientific and technological advances.

Confirmations of attendance have been received from the following: Oscar Arias, former president of Costa Rica; Ruud Lubbers, former prime minister of the Netherlands and chair of the World Wildlife Fund; Wally N'Dow, secretary-general of Habitat II in Istanbul; Her Majesty Queen Noor of Jordan; Lea Rabin, past first lady of Israel; Carol Bellamy, executive director of UNICEF; Alan Cranstan, former U.S. senator; John Nasbitt, futurist; Jane Nelson, policy and research director for the Prince of Wales Business Leaders Forum; Sir Shridath Ramphal, co-chair for the Commission on Global Governance; Steven Rockefeller, chair of Earth Charter International Drafting Committee; Anita Roddick, chair of the Body Shop International, friend of Prince Charles, and part of the PWBLF; Ismail Serageldin, vice-president of special programs at the World Bank; and Maurice Strong, the name a few. Additional speakers include: Catherine Burger, president of World Zoroastrian Cultural Foundation; Dr. Ross Jackson, chairman of Gaia Trust; Rev. Peter Kuzmic, professor of world missions at Gordon-Conwell Seminary; Malcolm McIntosh, director of the business school at the Centre for Corporate Citizenship, U.K.; and Ian Pearce, director of strategy and development at Business in the Community, U.K.

Themes include: "The New Economy Meets Sustainable Business," "Natural Capitalism," "Population Housing and Sustainable Development," "The Earth Charter," "Globalization and the New World Order," "The Future of Global Governance," "Trafficking in Small Arms," "The Future of Human Health and Happiness," and "Biotechnology, the Human Genome, the Human Being" are some of the numerous workshops.

As you can see, the work of the Prince of Wales Business Leaders Forum is quite extensive and literally "earth shattering." This puts a different light on the prince. He is emerging as more than a powerful world leader—he may be *THE* world leader of all time.

The Pope and the Queen on Equal Footing

Introduction

On March 15, Focus on the Family joined an alliance of evangelicals, Catholics, Muslims, and Mormons to defend the Catholic Church at the United Nations, where its UN status has come under attack by pro-abortion organizations as a result of its pro-life activities. The move to eliminate the Holy See's observer status has been under attack for years and goes back to the 1994 UN Conference on Population and Development in Cairo. In New York, the coalition presented a "historic Declaration in Support of the Holy See at the United Nations," which was signed by nearly eight hundred organizations from fifty countries. Tom Minnery, vice president of public policy at Focus on the Family, said, "*We Christians from all denominations* will stand with our Catholic allies to see that the abortion industry is not successful at silencing the Holy See at the UN" (emphasis added).

I find this quite puzzling. Just what message is Focus on the Family or any other conservative group trying to send? Ecumenicalism? Support for world government? More importantly, where will it lead? I believe that abortion is not the *issue* but the *reason* for this ecumenical alliance. The real issue is the quest for world government and world religion. The institution called the Catholic Church, which I believe is different from those who are believers in the tenets of the Catholic faith, is pitted directly against that of the British monarchy for the position of "king of the hill." The goals and objectives of the Catholic Church are precisely those of the United Nations. If you believe that it is the British royal family as the power behind the United Nations, then you have a very interesting scenario. Before you determine what man/woman or organization to follow, you had better understand the facts not seen.

The only two people in the world who share the same status, power, and position are the pope and the queen. As you will see, the Papal See is considered by the world's oldest authority on royalty, the *Almanach de Gotha,* to be the oldest monarchy in the world. Therefore, that makes the pope a king, with the cardinals of the church considered to be equal to the sons of kings, the head of a world religion, and the ruler of a recognized country, the Vatican. The queen comes from the world's second oldest monarchy, is the head of the Anglican Church, and is the ruler of Britain, as her titles show that the army, navy, and air force of the United Kingdom report to her. They are literally "Her Majesty's Army," "Her Majesty's Navy," and "Her Majesty's Air Force." What you are about to learn is that the apparent goals and objectives of both of these dynasties are not what they appear to be. It is the hidden which reveals their true nature and goal.

Background

As a result of covering the UN's Conference on the Environment and Population in Cairo in 1994, I was very impressed that the Catholic Church not only sent reporters from Catholic newspapers from around the world, but also sent money and materials to oppose population reduction. This was more than the evangelical church, which is ignorant of the international agenda, did. Those of us evangelicals who were there paid our own way and went as a result of individual leading from God. In Cairo, the Vatican specifically stated pro-life beliefs, which I hold. In return, I helped Catholic representatives distribute material to delegates so they could understand the real population reduction agenda. I saw the invisible hand of God work through an estimated one hundred eighty-five Catholics, fourteen non-Catholics, one Mormon, and one Muslim as we tried to hold back the insidious agenda of population reduction. Unfortunately, we were undone by a "higher power"—the World Bank—which announced at a press briefing that, in the future, countries seeking the World Bank's financial help would not get it unless they showed they were reducing their population.

My initial impression of the Holy See was changed, however, during a final press briefing. There, Catholic spokesman Dr. Joaquin Navaroo Vails stated the church's support for the United Nations' Programme of Action. I realized then that it supports world government through the United Nations by wearing both a "governmental hat," since the Vatican is a sovereign country, and a "religious hat," by seeking morality. Unfortunately, this impression has been reinforced by the Vatican's support of subsequent United Nations conferences held in Copenhagen (the Social Summit), Beijing (the Fourth Women's Conference), Istanbul (Habitat II) and Rome (the World Food Summit). If that is the case, then Catholic leaders are using the pro-life message to protect their real geo-political and geo-religious agenda—world government and world religion.

The defense of the Catholic Church's status at the United Nations shows how ignorant conservatives are with regard to the real purpose of the United Nations and its quest for world government, or "global governance," as it is called. It also shows conservative naivete with regard to the history and goals of the Roman Catholic Church. While I have Catholic friends whom I consider very devout and deep in their faith—in fact, some of them are more sensitive than some of my evangelical friends—this issue is about an institution that is recognized as a church, but which has left its first love. The institution of the Catholic

Church wants to exert its own power and be the winner in the end game for world control.

The *Almanach de Gotha*

In 1999, the *Almanach de Gotha* was published for the first time since World War II as a result of the reunification of Germany and the restoration of rights to the historic title. From 1763 to 1944, the *Gotha* was the ultimate authority on the reigning and formerly reigning houses of Europe. The *Almanach* primarily focuses on families whose ancestry can be traced back to the Holy Roman Empire (A.D. 936–1804), which was an effort to restore the Roman Republic (509–27 B.C.) and the Roman Empire (26 B.C.–A.D. 363). We must remember that all of Europe was under feudalism, which means only the most powerful or cunning were entitled to lands, castles, and titles.

King Juan Carlos I of Spain is the president of the Societe des Amis de l'Almanach de Gotha (Society of Friends of the Almanach de Gotha), King Michael I of Romania is chairman, and Prince Eduard, Duke of Anhalt, and Prince Karl-Emich (Furst) de Leningen serve as deputy chairmen. The Comite de Patronage (Committee of Patrons) includes Archduke Dr. Otto von Habsburg, Crown Prince Osman VI of Turkey, Prince Napoleon, Prince Dom Pedro Orleans-Bragance, along with thirteen other royal personages from all over Europe. This book has been described as one of the most important books for recognizing and knowing those who are truly royal. If your name is not in this book, you aren't royal!

The *Almanach* is divided into two parts: Part One, "Families," appears to contain the more important royal families that are reigning sovereign houses, described as "Genealogies of the Sovereign Houses of Europe and South America," while Part Two "Families" lists German and some non-German non-sovereign princely and ducal houses. This part is described as "Genealogies of the Mediatized Princes and Princely Counts of Europe and the Holy Roman Empire." "Mediatized sovereign houses" applies only to certain families that "occupied territories within the Holy Roman Empire. and its successor states in what is now considered modern Germany and Austria. The latrin root of the word "mediatized" is *media,* meaning "between," and its use comes from the number of layers of allegiance (in a feudal sense) between a nobleman and his suzerain. In the Holy Roman Empire, the ultimate feudal superior was the emperor, elected by the great electors. An "immediate" fief was held by feudal tenure directly from the emperor, with no intervening superior lord. When such a fief was placed under the authority of a feudal superior other than the emperor, and that superior was himself a tenant within the empire, this fief was "mediatized." According to the *Almanach,* "several hundred such 'immediate' states existed under the Holy Roman Empire." Duke and Prince Jean Engelbert d'Arenberg has explained this as follows:

> The Imperial States (Reichssande) were the real pillars of the Holy Roman Empire. They consisted mainly of the princes and counts of the Empire who possessed immediate territories therein; i.e., fiefs that were held directly of the Emperor himself, and who had, each of them, a vote and a seat in the Imperial Diet. The holders of these Imperial States and all those who were of equal birth with them constituted the High Nobility.[1]

In Part One, the countries listed include Albania, Andorra, Austria, Baden, Bavaria, Belgium, Bourbon-Orleans, Bourbon Parma, Bourbon-Two Scillies, Brazil, Bulgaria, Denmark, Great Britain, and Northern Ireland, Greece, Hanover, Hesse, Hohenzollern, Italy, Leichtenstein, Luxembourg, Mecklenburg, Monaco, the Netherlands, Norway, Oldenburg, Portugal, Prussia, Romania, Russia, Saxony, Spain, Sweden, Turkey, Yugoslavia/Serbia, the Sovereign Military Hospitalier Order of Malta, and the Holy See. While we would expect to see the reigning rulers of Monaco (Prince Ranier), Belgium (King Albert II), Denmark (Queen

Margareth II), Great Britain and Northern Ireland (Queen Elizabeth II), and a few others, perhaps we should ask ourselves why the Holy See is listed among "Reigning Sovereign Houses"? Since when? Have we missed something? Let's see what the foremost authority on royalty says.

The Holy See—also called the Papal See or sometimes the Holy Apostolic See—is the See of Saint Peter of Bethsaida in Galilee, Prince of the Apostles, personally established in Rome in the first century of Christianity having received from Jesus Christ the *suprema potestas pontificia* to be transmitted to his Successors. Besides its dignity of Patriarch of the West, the Universal Primacy of the Petrine See within the Church founded by Christ, as well as its sovereignty have been recognized from earliest times, also before the fall of the Roman Empire. The successors of Saint Peter form the uninterrupted line of Popes until today. The Incumbent of the Holy See is usually considered by Christian sovereign families as the "Father of the Family of Kings"; also since **His Holiness represents the oldest Monarchy in Europe**. Charlemagne, first Emperor of the Holy Roman Empire (800–806), was crowned in Rome on Christmas eve 799/800 by Pope Saint Leo III (795–816) [Pope Leo came from the powerful and ruthless Medici family]. Countless other Sovereigns have received their original or later investiture or anointment during their coronation from the Pope or his Legates. Today, many sovereigns or Heads of State inform the Pope of their succession and other events concerning their families. Besides purely ecclesiastical conferments or confirmations of dignities, all popes, since the early Middle Ages, have granted nobility also outside of their immediate civil or temporal jurisdiction. The triple sovereignty of His Holiness the Pope in Person, the Holy See, and of the State of Vatican City, although united, are therefore understood as distinct in law and practice.

International law recognizes the sovereignty [not being subject to anyone on earth] of the Pope, which is triple: personal, as Incumbent of the Holy See which itself is sovereign, and as Sovereign of the State of Vatican City [ruler of a country]. His Holiness personally sends Cardinal Legates and Cardinal Envoys, Apostolic Nuncios or Apostolic Delegates principally as the Incumbent of the Holy See, while the sovereign State of Vatican City is a member of many international organizations. As far as honors conferred by the Holy See are concerned, the *Almanach de Gotha* traditionally confines itself to the College of Cardinals since **its members are considered as princes of the Church, equal to the sons of reigning monarchs**, as well as citizens of the State of Vatican City if residing in Rome.

The Papacy being considered the oldest monarchy in Christendom, the sovereign (or Supreme) Pontiff is its first Monarch and hence customarily is called by other titles and addressed as *Most Holy Father* or *Your Holiness* or sometimes *Most August Pontiff*[2] [emphasis added].

According to the *Almanach,* the description and titles of Pope John Paul II are: "His Holiness Pope John Paul II sovereign Pontiff, Bishop of Rome, Vicar of Rome, Vicar of Jesus Christ, Successor of the Prince of the Apostles, Supreme Pontiff of the Church Universal, Patriarch of the West, Primate of Italy, Archbishop and Metropolitan of the Roman Province, Sovereign of the State of Vatican City, Servante of the *servants of God.*"[3]

The Vatican is guided by the Sacred College, which consists of three orders and is the pope's and Universal Church's senate. While there are a few exceptions, cardinals are consecrated bishops, using their episcopal titles only if belonging to the Cardinalitial Order of Bishops or Priests. Interestingly enough, they are considered

as Roman Princes [all considered equal to princes of

the blood royal of any country; that means equal to "Bonnie Prince Charles"!] they follow immediately after the reigning Sovereign Pontiff and rank with the Princes of reigning Houses. Cardinal Legates a latere represent the Sovereign Pontiff in Person and are never outranked, being during their mission on equality with Emperors and Kings, or other Heads of States, all addressed as "Brothers or Sisters," this being constantly recognized since 1157. Cardinal Envoys are outranked only by Heads of State [emphasis added].[4]

This information puts the Vatican in a whole new light, even though there is no blood line from Peter—the pope is considered equal with royalty and answers to no one on earth. Does this mean each diocese is equal to the fiefdoms of the temporal monarchies? In addition, the Vatican can take mere men and make them royal—equal to the princes of the reigning houses? How can the United Nations even consider throwing out the Holy See? Do they not know who they are dealing with?

Aristrocracy
One of the old line aristocratic families in Europe dating back to 962 and the Holy Roman Empire, are the Frescobaldis of Florence, Italy.

In their time the Frescobaldi family have been knights in armour, merchants, bankers, and counsellors to the Kings of England [1294–1311], tax collectors for the Pope, musicians, scholars, poets, and explorers; they have plotted murder, been sent into exile, been publicly executed and they have gone bankrupt at least twice.

Dino Frescobaldi says this: "What matters about aristocracy is influence, power, and money. Culture, pedigree, and tradition are also important, of course, but without power and money, titles are meaningless."[5]

British Royalty—A Comparison

I have long been fascinated with royalty. In fact, I thought when I was twelve years old I might marry Prince Charles. We must ask ourselves what royalty is. Basically, royals are ranked by how long they have been "king of the hill" (my personal description for their power and position). For example, in Britain, those who are dukes and lors today basically did the king's business five to nine hundred years ago, and, in return, the king granted them titles, lands, and castles that have made them exceedingly rich and powerful, since they have retained their original feudalistic holdings. In return for their continued assistance throughout the centuries, royals have been given various additional awards that help maintain their longevity and positions of prominence and favor with the monarch. The king, in return, was made king because of the loyalty of these dukes, lords, and knights, who fought for him and furthered his kingdom. Without such support, the king would not have sustained his position as king and expanded his territory and rulership in the way and manner in which he did. Over the centuries, nobility established elaborate ceremonies to give their power a "mystical" aura; they put on airs of importance over the common man, who is not "noble" and who cannot compete with the power of crowns, robes, and grand ceremonies.

My book, *Prince Charles: The Sustainable Prince* explains the role of the British royal family as the major power behind the United Nations. This concept, coupled with the understanding that the Holy See considers itself the oldest monarchy in the world, reveals another aspect of the race for who will be supreme "king of the world." The British royal family is the hidden power behind the United Nations, while the Holy See wants to unite the world spiritually to support its own political power. This all becomes extremely interesting when you realize that the only other person in the world with the same functions and position as the pope is Queen Elizabeth. While the pope's monarchy is eight hundred years older than that of the queen's, both are rulers of countries—most people do not know that the British army, navy, and air force are directly under her command (which, in my opinion, makes her the true ruler, not the prime minister), and when Henry VIII broke with the Roman Catholic Church, the royal family became the head of the Church of England!! Furthermore, if the recent movie *Elizabeth* has any validity or truth to it, they bring out the fact that Queen Elizabeth I was referred to as the "Virgin Queen" to imply or make a comparison between herself and Mary, the mother of Jesus whom the Catholic Church worships.

Royal Orders
Britain's Queen Elizabeth II gives gifts to those whom she wishes to honor and also on the recommendation of the prime minister. These come in two ways: Orders of Knighthood and Order of Merit (good works). The Order of the Garter is the most famous and most coveted Order of Knighthood. Others that rank next to it are the Order of the Thistle (the Scottish equivalent to the Order of the Garter), the Order of Bath (Presidents Ronald Reagan and George Bush, General Dwight Eisenhower, and General George Patton have received this award), and the Order of Merit, which is reserved for those who have outstanding achievements in the fields of science, medicine, the arts, literature, and politics. Other lesser orders include the Order of St. Michael and St. George, for diplomats, ambassadors, and Foreign Office (equivalent to the U.S. State Department) figures, the Royal Victorian Order, which is the personal gift of the sovereign, and the Order of St. John of Jerusalem, to name a few.[6] When a person is not of noble birth, they can be knighted but are made a "companion."

The Order of the Garter was created in 1348 by King Edward

II and has its own motto, history, and crowning ceremonies. Interestingly enough, its insignia is a red cross, which is called St. George's Cross. Knights are given a jeweled collar, which is quite elaborate and has St. George on a white stallion with a spear in his hand that has been thrust through the mouth of the dragon (do you think this is **the** dragon of Revelation 12 and 13?). This medallion was inspired by the tale of King Arthur and the Knights of the Round Table. I have noted that most of the official portraits of the queen (and previous kings) show the sovereign wearing this collar. When I was in Scotland last year, I saw it in a museum. It is absolutely spectacular, as the front of it is set in large diamonds while the back is in lacquer and vividly depicts St. George, the stallion, and the dragon. What I realized as I was looking at it is that the diamond side is what the public sees, while the back is hidden to anyone who is not a knight and thus the true meaning is hidden. The Order meets in St. George's Chapel at Windsor once a year, where business is conducted and new knights are inducted. I visited the chapel and find it to be quite interesting and mysterious, a result of the Order's secrecy from the common man.

It is the goal of all British nobility to work for the furtherance of the British kingdom so that the sovereign will recognize their achievements and award them accordingly. Because it is considered to be a designation of great power and accomplishment, Princess Diana's most profound wish was to be given the Order of the Garter. When a person of royal standing is named in the *Almanach de Gotha,* also listed are the orders (knighthoods) that they have received from their own sovereign and other sovereigns. The number and source of awards denotes a person's importance. When you see pictures of Prince Philip or Prince Charles in full dress, they will usually have a chest full of medals. Most of these are the various orders they have been awarded and reflect their esteemed position in royal circles.

This introduction to the various orders of the British Empire is given because the Holy See also bestows its own orders on those who have supported and promoted the work of the Catholic Church. All of this, then, presents a different picture that we normally don't read about.

Catholic Orders

Several years ago, I began searching about knighthood and royal orders. I ordered two books, one of which was *Orders of Knighthood and Merit*. When the book came, not only was it huge and very expensive, but it wasn't exactly what I was looking for. As I paged through it, I realized that it was about the Catholic orders, a subject that I was not familiar with and which surprised me. As I read about the Catholic Church giving out the kind of royal orders that royal families award, I was puzzled. When I read the *Almanach de Gotha* and learned that the Catholic Church is considered the oldest monarchy in the world, the puzzle pieces started to come together.

It is very interesting that most of the various royal orders have their foundation either in the idea of King Arthur and the Knights of the Round Table or in the Crusades to the Holy Land during the beginning of the second millennium. For example, the Most Noble Order of the Golden Fleece (the Royal House of Habsburg-Lorraine)

> recalls the Greek legend of the Golden Fleece captured by Jason from the dragon, symbolizing Jerusalem which, in the original Crusader spirit, the Order was to win back for Christendom from the Muslims. Since the reign of Philip the Handsome, the symbolic interpretation of Jason was no longer used because of its Greek pagan connotations. Bishop Gillaume Filastre, Chancellor of the Order, gave six new references for the symbolic use of the fleece: Jason, Gideon, Jacob, Mesa, Job, and David. Each of these fleeces represented one of the virtues with which a true knight should be endowed: magnanimity, justice, prudence, loyalty, patience, and clemency.[7]

The papacy has not only encouraged the foundation of secular Orders of Knighthood under its auspices or patronage, but there is a history of popes founding Pontifical Orders of Knighthood and Orders of Merit, besides countless crosses and medals. Pontifical Orders of Knighthood are in the personal gift of the pope. All Pontifical Equestrian Orders belong in the category of Orders of Merit. The order of precedence is: The Supreme Order of Christ, which is reserved for Christian heads of state, the Order of the Gold Spur (or of the Golden Militia), which is to be conferred on heads of state who had to confess the Christian, not necessarily the Catholic, religion, and the Golden Collar of the Pian Order, which is open to all heads of state, regardless of their religious affiliation. Each Order has its own criteria and prerequisites for converment.[8]

With each of these Orders comes a special outfit to match—either a tux or a special uniform, along with the cross, collar, and star (the same thing applies to the British royal Orders—each has a special uniform or robe). "The purpose for most of the Catholic-founded Orders is: the defense of the belief in the Immaculate Conception of the Blessed Virgin Mary and her motherhood of God, and the divinity of Christ."[9] Most recently I saw a picture of new priests laying prostrate, which was described as paying homage to the pope—it did not clarify if the homage was to the Lord God Creator of Heaven and earth, or to the pope as pope, king, head of state, or all three.

Most interestingly, the recently deceased son of President Kennedy inherited noble rank on the death of his grandfather, Joseph P. Kennedy in 1969.[10] According to *American Presidential Families,* his grandmother, Rose Kennedy, was not only

created a papal countess by Pius XII (himself the holder of an elective office, which, like the American presidency, combines the headshuip of both state and government); even in little things there were royal parallels. There was the countess's insistence that no two Kennedy offspring should fly in the same airplane, so like the safety rules governing members of the British royal family. There was Jack Kennedy's habit of carrying no cash on his person, so like that of the Queen of England. Even if actual royal rank eluded the Kennedy's, they were undoubtedly noble. Rose's title of countess—the only rank of its kind created by Pius XII during his entire reign—was conferred on her for her life only. But when Joe Kennedy attended Pius XII's coronation in early 1939 he was created a Knight Grand Cross of the Order of Pius IX, which still conferred hereditary nobility by male primogeniture on its grantee and his successors."[11]

The Goals and Objectives of the Catholic Church
The Catholic Church
For most Protestants, the history of the Catholic Church is one of oppression and control—as well as distortion of the Word of God. While the paint from Michaelangelo's brush was drying on the ceiling of the Sistine Chapel (1512), Martin Luther was nailing his "95 Theses" on the Castle Church door in Wittenburg in 1517. This was done in protest to the sale of indulgences by the Catholic Church in Rome, which enabled anyone who had the money to "buy salvation," while those who did not or who could not afford the indulgences were out of luck. The selling of indulgences was an idea developed to help the church raise money, as they usually borrowed from the Rothschilds or Morgans at usurious rates. Pope Leo "squander[ed] the resources of the Holy See on carnivals, war, gambling, and the chase."[12] The Catholics view the Protestant revolt (protest) against papal authority as shattering the religious unity of Europe.

Interestingly enough, Catholics credit the loss of the church's power (perhaps we should ask when the Catholic Church left its first love of God?) with helping it develop its innate "geo-religious capacity. It developed a diplomatic style that relied principally on moral status. It developed the Catholic sense of the papacy as the ultimate arbiter for problems and dilemmas affecting nations all over the globe."[13] In today's terms we would call this reinventing the church. The headlines with regard to the pope's visit to Israel read, "In Holy Land, Pope Was a Devout Diplomat."[14]

The Pope

Pope John Paul is the two hundred sixty-fourth pope of the Roman Catholic Church, and the first from a communist country. At his election it was said, "Cardinal Wojtyla can lead to cooperation between the two ideologies: Marxism and Christianity."[15] He is the most traveled pope in history and has become a power in and of his own making.

The Goal

According to Malachi Martin, the late author of *The Keys of This Blood,* the world is "involved in an all-out, no-holds-barred, three-way global competition about who will establish the first one-world system of government that has ever existed in the society of nations."[16] When Martin wrote his book in 1990, he said there were three contenders: John Paul himself, Mikhail Gorbachev, who at the time was the leader of the USSR, and a group of globalist contenders comprised of transnationalists (multinational and transnational corporations) and internationalists (national and international governmental leaders). Martin said that the goals all three had in common were "individual freedom and cultural rights, and the good life to which each individual has a fundamental right."[17] Interestingly enough, all of these goals match those of the United Nations. In fact, James Wolfensohn, president of the World Bank, traveled to London in 1998 and met with the Bishop of Canterbury in his home, Lambeth Palace, to work with major world faiths to eradicate hunger and poverty and overcome mutual suspicions of the past. Out of that meeting came the agreement to set up a working group that would identify five or six projects that the development experts and world leaders could work on together. It should be noted that Pope Paul has met with all of the leaders of the major religions to achieve peace.

Martin points out that none of the above goals are rooted in the moral laws of human behavior. Gorbachev is a Leninist "devoted to achieving the goals of Leninism and the worldwide Leninist association of all workers under the banner of Marxism."[18] Martin goes on to describe the pope's goal:

> The sociocultural model is based on Thomas Aquina seven hundred years ago to the effect that the two loves of any individual human being are the love of God and the love of one's native country, and further, that these can live and flourish only within the framework of a religious nationalism.[19]

The solidarity movement in Poland was the Catholic Church's first experiment with religious nationalism, as it was created by them to oppose communism.

Ten years ago the newly elected pope gave an address that provided the

> broad philosophic and quasi-theological umbrella beneath which secularism within the Roman Church would be protected from the storm of protest and outrage mounted by traditional Catholics in the years following the council. Pope Paul VI said the church had decided to opt for man; to serve man, to help him build his home on this earth. Man with his ideas and his aims, man with his hopes and his fears, man in his difficulties and suffering—that was the centerpiece of the church's interest, said the Pontiff to his bishops.[20]

Paul VI's emphasis on human interest became the basis for discarding sacrifice and prayer and faith and the Sacraments of the church as the watchwords of hope in this world. **They were replaced by human solidarity**. Ecumenicalism was a means not a genuine healing but of leveling differences of whatever kind between all Christian believers and nonbelievers. That fit nicely with the new central aim of human solidarity as the hope of mankind. The fundamental struggle in which the church and all Catholics were engaged was no longer the personal war between Christ as Savior and Lucifer as the Cosmic Adversary of the Most High in the quest for men's souls. The struggle was no longer on the supernatural plane at all, in fact. It was in the material circumstances of the tangible, socio-political here and now. It was the class struggle Marx and Lenin had propounded as the only worthwhile combat zone for humans.[21]

Execution of the Plan

With regard to the execution of the plan, I think it is safe to say that once the churches unite under a common banner, there will be a "leveling out of differences" that will provide a new interdependency among the religions. This is the "right flank" of the united religions movement. The "left flank" is the environmental, New Age, Eastern religions. I find it most interesting that Prince Charles, who is an environmentalist and New Ager, as future head of the Church of England, wants to be considered the "Defender of Faiths" instead of the "Defender of the Faith." Consider the following:

United Nations Agenda. The human solidarity goals of the Roman Catholic Church are the same as the goals and objectives of the United Nations. Please read the Programmes of Action for the conferences held in Rio de Janeiro, Copenhagen, Cairo, Beijing, Istanbul, and Rome. Furthermore, the Holy See does not actually buck the UN agenda, but *appears* to buck its agenda. In Cairo, where Catholics protested the language in several sections of the Programme of Action, they gave in because

despite reservations, it agreed with the basic objectives of paragraph 8.25 which calls on governments to provide health services for women suffering from complications of abortion and to assure that abortions are safe "in circumstances in which abortion is not against the law." The Vatican said it could not endorse the concept of "legal abortion" and reserved its right to speak further when the section comes up for final approval in the Plendary.[22]

The compromise that was finally agreed to over abortion was to change the term to fit the Vatican's definition. This is in line with all of the word twisting the Vatican has done from its inception. Peter, as the first Catholic pope, was married and furthermore, he never writes in his two New Testament books that he is establishing a spiritual monarchy, but does discuss apostasy in severe terms in Second Peter 2:20–22. Peter makes it quite clear that for those who escape the pollution of this world through knowledge of Jesus Christ, and then return to the world, it had been better for them not to have known the way of righteousness than to have then turned from the holy commandment delivered unto them. He uses the analogy of a dog returning to its own vomit!

United World Religions. I interviewed the Rev. Bishop Swing of Grace Episcopal Cathedral in San Francisco during the UN's fiftieth anniversary celebrations in 1995. He told me that he was looking to bring together all of the world's major religions to have a type of "UN of world religions." He has done that, and now there is great activity to unite the major religions in order to have "world peace through world law with justice." In November 1999, the World Federalist Association, Chesapeake Region, hosted a one-day conference on "The Search for World Peace and Justice: What Can World Religions Do?" According to Carl Telchrib, the Roman Catholic perspective was provided by Dr. John Logue, senior vice-president of the World Federalist Association and a practicing Roman Catholic. Dr. Logue stated: "We must work as hard as we can to build a world commonwealth, a United Nations world commonwealth, which has the power to enact, interpret, and enforce world law—limited world law on individuals—on you and on me." He also explained "that Pope Pius XII and John XXIII agree" with the doctrines of the World Federalists for world government.[23]

The Evangelical-Catholic Accord. On March 29, 1994, nine months before the United Nations Conference on Population and Development, the Associated Press reported:

> Catholics and evangelicals are asking their flocks for a remarkable leap of faith: to finally accept each other as Christians. . . .
> In what's being called a historic declaration, evangelicals including Pat Robertson and Charles Colson joined with conservative Roman Catholic leaders Tuesday in upholding the ties of faith that bind the nation's largest and most politically active religious groups.[24]

The "Evangelicals and Catholics Together: The Christian Mission in the Third Millennium" statement says: "in the last generation, it has become common for evangelicals and Catholics to work together on issues such as abortion, pornography, vouchers for religious education, and voluntary school prayer."[25] A year later, Pope John Paul II issued a one hundred fifteen-page encyclical, "'That They All May Be One,' which is dedicated to the search for unity among Christian churches that split from each other during the past thousand years." Commenting on the encyclical, Cardinal Edward Cassidy said: "The pope sees the Catholic position on primacy as an essential point of faith. . . . The pope made it clear he would not accept a symbolic papacy without teeth and that Rome would have to hold the primary place among Christians."[26]

Conclusion

Abortion is not the issue but the mechanism through which to find "human solidarity" politically, religiously, culturally, and historically. At the World Food Summit in Rome in November 1996, Cardinal Angelo Sodano (don't forget, he is equal to a prince in status) outlined the Holy See's support for the United Nations Programmes of Action. He said:

> It is a question of solidarity lived in the light of certain basic principles: (1) The first principle of our commitment to solidarity is respect for every human person. (2) The second principle is that of solidarity. If individual human beings possess their own inalienable dignity, when they need our help we are bound to give it to them. (3) A third principle inspiring our social activity is that of the universal designation of the goods of the earth. In using them, a man should regard his lawful possession not merely as his own but also as common property in the sense that they should accrue to the benefit of not only himself but others. (4) A fourth principle inspiring the Holy See's activity in the international sphere is the promotion of peace.

It appears that with the embracing of our humanistic goal, which displaces Jesus Christ, this Catholic church has lost sight of its true spiritual purpose and has chosen a worldly one. Lastly, the *London Daily Mail* reported that Buckingham Palace is considering having all of the faiths which reside in England present at Charles future coronation where he will become "Defender of the Faiths."

Notes

1. John Kennedy, editor and publisher, *Almanach de Gotha, Original Genealogical Reference 1763–1999, 183rd edition* (London: John Kennedy, 1999), 862.
2. Ibid., 147–149.
3. Ibid., 149–150.
4. Ibid., 149–151.
5. Robert Lacey, *Aristocrats* (London: Hutchinson and Co. Ltd.,

1983), 19, 21.

6. Hugo Vickers, *Royal Orders: The Honours and the Honoured* (London: Boxtree Limited, 1994), 9–10.

7. Peter Bander van Duren, *Orders of Knighthood and of Merit: The Pontifical, Religious and Secularised Catholic-founded Orders, and Their Relationship to the Apostolic See* (Buckinghamshire, England: Colin Smythe Limited, 1995), 244.

8. Ibid., 55–58.

9. Ibid., 51.

10. Hugh Brogan and Charles Mosley, *American Presidential Families* (New York: MacMillan Publishing, 1993), 674.

11. Ibid., 674.

12. Roland H. Bainton, *Here I Stand: A Life of Martin Luther* (Nashville: Abingdon Press, 1978), 56.

13. Malachi Martin, *The Keys of This Blood* (New York: Touchstone, 1990), 136.

14. Lee Hockstader, *Washington Post,* "In Holy Land, Pope Was a Devout Diplomat," March 28, 2000, A16.

15. Malachi Martin, *The Keys of This Blood*, 93.

16. Ibid., 1.

17. Ibid., 19.

18. Ibid., 32.

19. Ibid., 50.

20. Ibid., 259.

21. Ibid., 260.

22. Jack Freeman, *The Earth Times,* "Breakthrough Is Reported on Abortion Issues," September 10, 1994, 1.

23. Carl Telchrib, *Hope for the World,* "Conforming the Church to the New Millennium," Winter 2000, 6–7.

24. Noah Hutchings, *Prophetic Observer,* "Strange Pew Fellows?" May 1994, 1.

25. Ibid., 1.

26. Noah Hutchings, *Prophetic Observer,* "Papal Infallibility: A Pre-Condition for Church Unity," July 1995, 1.

Appendix E

Gorby and the Prince

While many think Prince Charles is a lost soul who is looking for purpose and meaning in life, the fact that one of his organizations, The Prince's Trust, is cosponsoring the Gorbachev State of the World Forum in September should signal, if nothing else, his "coming out" party.

For years there has been a media blackout as to the real role which Prince Charles plays in world affairs. In this regard, the prince is a military leader, head of state in his own right, an activist on the world stage, and a one worlder/environmentalist.

Military Leader

Charles is a complex man with many sides. He is a man of action, having served in the Royal Navy in a number of junior and senior command positions. According to one of his biographers, William Holden, he is a helicopter pilot and has logged over nine hundred hours flying a wide variety of jet fighter planes, including the Chipmunk, Spitfire, Nimrod, Phantom, Jet Provost, and Harrier T4, to name a few. The prince holds the rank of Colonel-in-Chief of seventeen regiments in addition to having served in the Royal Navy. When he turned fifty, the prince was promoted to a two-star rank in all three services of the armed forces. He is commissioned into the army as a Major General and holds the ranks of Rear Admiral in the Royal Navy and Air Vice Marshal in the Royal Air Force.

Head of State

While many think Charles will become head of state when he inherits the British throne, that is not so. In 1969, he was crowned Prince of Wales in Caernarvon Castle in Wales, which is a principality, like Monaco or Lichenstein, of its own. When the queen was crowned, woven into her coronation robes were the symbols of England, Scotland, and Ireland. Since Wales has its own ruler, the Prince of Wales, the red dragon which is its symbol was not included. This should put Charles in a different light. He does not have to wait for the throne of England to become a head of state. As a result of his lineage and birth, he automatically is one. However, through his various trusts and through the Prince of Wales Business Leaders Forum, he now becomes a man of action, cementing his global leadership position.

Activist

The prince has numerous social/environmental/governmental activities. He is president of Business in the Community, The Prince's Foundation and The Prince's Trust, to name a few of his trusts. He also initiated, organized, and oversees the Prince of Wales Business Leaders Forum.

The Prince's Trust

Set up in 1976 by the prince, its goal is to help young people succeed by providing opportunities which they would not have otherwise. It provides help with raising educational achievements, training, business start-up advice and loans, and financial support. It has over eleven thousand volunteers and a staff of over four hundred professionals. There are over three hundred community-based personal development courses throughout the United Kingdom. In 1996, The Prince's Trust consolidated The Prince's Trust, The Prince's Youth Business Trust, The Prince's Trust Volunteers, and The Prince of Wales Committee.

The Prince of Wales Business Leaders Forum

While the philanthropic activities of the prince are well known, his reinventing government is not. Of the two major biographies written to commemorate his fiftieth birthday two years ago, one barely mentioned the Prince of Wales Business Leaders Forum (PWBLF). In 1990, Charles called together over one hundred global business leaders to come together in Charleston, South Carolina, to work together to promote socially responsible business practices. While this all sounds noble, it is not. Prince Charles, along with the Forum's top fifty international corporate members—Diego, SmithKline Beecham, Coca-Cola, Levi Strauss, Rio Tinto, BP-Amoco, Asea Brown Boveri (ABB), 3M, BMW, TRW, and Shell, along with The Perot Group, Turner Broadcasting, and others, are setting up public-private partnerships throughout the world.

A public-private partnership is a partnership (business arrangement) between government and business, along with nongovernmental organizations who perform the daily chores of the partnership. The word *public* refers to government—local, county, state, federal, and international levels of government—while *private* refers to nongovernmental groups such as foundations, nonprofits, corporations, and individuals. Another word for this marriage is fascism. This new partnership arrangement has been the focus of the UN Habitat II Conference in 1996 which encouraged public-private partnerships. Al Gore's "Reinventing Government" program, and the new forms of government now being implemented by countries worldwide. Interestingly enough, our new form of government in the U.S. is being changed to public-private partnerships! The downsizing of government has shifted responsibility from governmental to these new partnerships. For example, when a public-private partnership owns your sewer facility, that asset has just transferred from government to this new partnership! As a taxpayer, you not only lose an asset but the objective of that partnership changes from service to profit!

World Government Environmentalist

The side of Charles which is being unveiled at the Gorbachev State of the World Forum is his world government/environmentalist philosophy. In an interview that he gave the BBC's "Newsnight" program in 1994, he expressed his devotion to his work for Britain and the Commonwealth. He said, "So much I try to do is behind the scenes so it is difficult for people to understand how all the things fit together." The actions and passions of the prince make him for world government and an environmentalist, both mutually interdependent.

In 1992 the United Nations sponsored the Conference on Environment and Development, now called the "Rio Earth Summit." There a very radical environmental agenda was unveiled—the effects of which are only now being felt and understood by the American people. In Rio the United Nations presented their new environmental philosophy by which the world should be governed which basically points in the direction of world government, i.e., the United Nations as caretaker of the world and its resources. This document, known as "Agenda 21," basically perverts Genesis 1 by insisting that the earth has dominance over man instead of man having dominance over the earth. This new philosophy is known as "Gaia," the worship of Mother Earth. It was Prince Charles who played a major "behind the scenes role" when he held a two-day international seminar in April 1991 aboard the royal yacht *Britannia,* moored off the coast of Brazil. His goal was to bring together key international figures in an attempt to achieve a degree of harmony between the conflicting attitudes of Europe, the United States, and the developing nations (led by Brazil).

Among others, he invited then-Senator Albert Gore, senior officials from the World Bank, chief executives from companies such as Shell and British Petroleum, principal nongovernmental organizations, and European politicians, including the British ministers of overseas aid and the environment.

The prince was an early supporter of sustainable development, which calls for the reduction of the world's population in order to protect resources for "future generations," even before it was introduced into Rio's Agenda 21 Programme!

The Gorbachev State of the World Forum

When you examine this conference, you will find that the themes correspond to the activities of the Prince of Wales which correspond to the goals and objectives of the United Nations! From September 4–10, the Forum is bringing together representatives from nation-states, international institutions, corporations, unions, major religions, academia, science and technology, and nongovernmental organizations for a "global town meeting." The Forum's belief is that "the future of global governance must include governments, civil society, and the private sector," which are the components of public-private partnerships. Borrowing from George Bush's "New World Order," Gorbachev will convene the opening plenary discussion on "Globalization and the New World Order." Does this tell you anything? Lastly, after eight years of deliberations, the Earth Charter, a common agreement for all humanity to protect (control) the environment and enforce sustainable development will be unveiled. This document was recently presented to Queen Beatrix of the Netherlands on June 29 in a special ceremony. As reported by AOL, "Today's presentation of the Earth Charter to Queen Beatrix and the people of the Netherlands marks a significant step toward one of the Earth Charter's goals—endorsed by the United Nations."

Those who have confirmed their attendance include Oscar Arias, Jean Bertrand-Aristide, Lea Rabin, Her Majesty Queen Noor of Jordan, and Sen. Alan Cranston. Those attending from the United Nations include Carol Bellamy (UNICEF), Wally N'Dow (UNCHS), Juan Somavia (ILO), and Carlos Magarinos (UNIDO). Representatives from the religious community include the World Zoroastrian Cultural Foundation, the Gaia Trust, and

Gordon-Conwell Seminary. Those affiliated with the Prince of Wales and his Business Leaders Forum include Jermyn Brocks from PriceWaterhouseCooper, Anita Roddick from The Body Shop International, Catherine Burger, Jane Nelson, and Michael Steward from PWBLF, J. Douglas Graham from KPMG Consulting, and Ian Pearce from Business in the Community.

It appears that all of the pieces with regard to the prince's activities are fitting together. There is an old adage, "Show me who your friends are, and I will tell you what you are." In this case, the future heir to the British throne appears to be positioning himself with a "winner take all" philosophy. His agenda is the same as the United Nations, and his friends espouse "global governance" which is nothing less than world government. Yes, it appears the prince is coming out of the closet. The question is which throne does he want?

Information on the Gorbachev State of the World Forum can be obtained through their website: *www.worldforum.org.*

Appendix F

A Chronology of the Prince of Wales and His Rise to World Leadership

1948   Born (November 14)

1958   Created Prince of Wales and Knight of the Garter

1965   Turns eighteen, which means he is able to succeed to the throne in his own right

1967   Joins Trinity College to read archaeology, anthropology, and history

1968   *June.* Invested as Knight of the Garter—officially joins the twenty-four Knights of the Order of the Garter, who are the Queen's inner confidants

   December. Chairs the Steering Committee for Wales, "The Countryside in 1970" Conference. The prince gives his first public speech on the environment, showing his concern for the preservation of natural habitats in the wild and the protection of the rural landscape, as well as discussing "the horrifying effects of pollution in all its forms," citing "oil pollution at sea, chemical pollution discharged from factories and chemical plants, and air pollution." (Dimbleby, 312)

1969 *July.* Invested as Prince of Wales at Caernarvon Castle—writes in his diary, "For me, by far the most moving and meaningful moment came when I put my hands between Mummy's and swore to be her liege man of life and limb and to live and die against all manner of folks—such magnificent, mediaeval, appropriate words, even if they were never adhered to in those old days." (Prince of Wales' diary from Dimbleby, 134)

1970 *February.* Attends the Council of Europe's European Conservation Conference in Strasbourg

June. Graduates from Cambridge

1971 Royal Navy

The Prince of Wales' Committee, established in 1971, has provided £3.2 million in grants to 3,533 voluntary groups working on projects to improve the environment of Wales. It now funds three hundred fifty projects each year.

1972 Royal Navy

1974 *January-August.* Serves aboard HMS *Jupiter*

1975 *March–June.* Serves aboard HMS *Hermes* commando ship with 845 Squadron ("Red Dragons")

December. Private visit as guest of Prince Bernard of the Netherlands (Bernard started the Bilderbergers)

1976 *February–December.* Commands HMS *Bronington* mine-hunter

The Prince's Trust established to help disadvantaged young people. By 1994 the trust had helped twelve thousand individuals with a program of grants and training through fourteen hundred volunteers. In 1994 its turnover was expected to exceed £10 million. In 1990 the Prince's Trust volunteers work in communities to show the value of "team building" and to work on a variety of community projects. Twelve governmental departments assist to expand the trust's reach.

1977 *March.* Ghana (official visit)—supposed to be where he got his *spiritual understanding*

October. Visits the United States and meets with President Nixon

Charles examines his own personal beliefs and starts to investigate "parapsychology," which is the occult. He writes to the University of Wales to establish a chair of parapsychology, "I am strongly of the opinion that such a chair would be of the greatest importance in advancing man's knowledge of a field that is given scant attention and yet is of immense significance in terms of the 'invisible' aspects of our existence in this universe." (Dimbleby, 248)

The Royal Jubilee Trust—established by the prince to help young people to help others in the community

1978 *November.* Brussels—official visit to NATO and SHAPE headquarters

1979   *April.* Visits the Lester B. Pearson College of the Pacific (one of the United World colleges) in British Columbia as president of the United World College (UWC). The UWC is founded on the teachings of Kurt Hahn, is based on international education, and accepts only the most promising students. It is considered a "teenage United Nations" and provides graduates with a two-year international baccalaureate. Programs are based on "new forms of thinking" to prepare students for the twenty-first century. (Interview by Joan Veon with UWC in United States, April 22, 1997)

1980   *January.* Switzerland—lunch in Zurich to mark sixtieth anniversary of British-Swiss Chamber of Commerce

Becomes patron of IT—the Intermediate Technology Development Group that was formed in 1965 by the author of one of his biographies, Jonathan Dimbleby. IT looks to develop means of production for the needs of people in the third world. (The President's Commission on Sustainable Development has an affiliation with IT through Al Gore.)

March–April. Visits Ottawa and British Columbia as president of UWC

1981   *March–April.* Visits New Zealand, Australia, and Venezuela as president of United World Colleges

April–May. Receives honorary fellowship from College of William and Mary

Establishes the Prince of Wales's Advisory Group on Disability and the Prince of Wales Community Venture

August. Marries Diana, Princess of Wales

Business in Community formed by a "maverick group of businessmen." These men hoped "to persuade major companies to donate sums of money, personnel, or resources to be invested in community trusts, projects, and, above all, local enterprise agencies. BiC would serve as a catalyst for local action, inspiring *partnerships* in projects rather than managing them; it would act as an honest broker—or in the vogue word, *'enabler'—between the companies and the communities they served, creating mutual goodwill as well as mutual advantage.* The notion of BiC had grown out of the 1980 Anglo-American Conference on Community Involvement chaired by Tom King, then-local government minister, at which British tycoons had heard of American success during the 1970s in persuading big business to help finance the regeneration of decaying, post-industrial cities [Pittsburgh]. The Toxteth [in Britain] riots changed all that. Given special responsibility for the area, then-Environment Minister Michael Heseltine took a busload of leading industrialists to see the bleak post-riot landscape for themselves. *Only by partnership, Heseltine argued, could a thriving community arise from these ashes with any effective speed. Urban development corporations would be set up around the country; tax incentives would be offered in the hope that the private sector would quadruple government contributions.* Chairmen and CEOs returned to their offices that day intent on getting their companies involved with the existing local government enterprise agencies, which soon became much more numerous . . ." (Holden, *King Charles III*, 145–6, [emphasis added]). Business in Community became the Prince of Wales Business Leaders Forum in 1990.

1982 *October.* Prince Charles opens the new United World College in Montezuma, New Mexico. His mentor, Armand Hammer, was instrumental in getting the college set up and established in New Mexico. Visits Lester B. Pearson College of the Pacific in British Columbia.

At a speech at the 150th birthday of the British Medical Association, the prince speaks about "his own immersion in the unconventional values of oriental culture, the writings of Jung, and the mystical revelations about the natural world he shared with Laurens van der Post." The prince was arguing for "holism." "Closely aligned to the psychology of Jung and to various reinterpretations of the structure of the natural world, explored by scientists like James Lovelock, who formulated the Gaia hypothesis, the concept of 'holism' (a term which brought a curl to the lips of scientific materialists) invoked the principles of harmony, balance and the interconnectedness of natural phenomena, combining them with the search for inner awareness" (Dimbleby, 306–7).

1984 *March.* Tours Tanzania, Zambia, Zimbabwe, and Botswana as director of the Commonwealth Development Corporation

May. In a speech at the 150th anniversary dinner of the Royal Institute of British Architecture, Charles criticizes modern architecture while elevating community architecture. "For far too long, it seems to me, some planners and architects have consistently ignored the feelings and wishes of the mass of ordinary people in this country. What I believe is important about community architecture is that it has 'shown' ordinary people that their views are worth having; that architects and planners do not necessarily have the monopoly of knowing what is best. . . . I express the earnest hope that the next one hundred fifty years will see a new harmony between imagination and taste and in the relationship between the architects and the people of this country" (Dimbleby, 316–17).

July. Attends the UWC gala in Monte Carlo

October. Visits Italy—United World College in Trieste, the United Nations Food and Agriculture Building in Rome, and the pope, where the prince and princess attend a "Celebration of Faith." "In the spring of 1982, the Pope visited Britain on a pastoral visit . . . where the Pope and the Archbishop of Canterbury knelt together in prayer in an historic act of reconciliation" in a service at Canterbury Catheral" (Dimbleby, 348–49).

1985 *September.* Becomes president of Business in Community, which was the originator of the "partnership" between business, government, and the community. It currently has four hundred fifty companies (eighty of which are the top one hundred corporations in Britain), eight regional offices, and five campaign teams. It has a turnover of £5 million. In 1989 the prince launched Business in the Environment to link twenty-nine hundred communities and fifty environmental networks to promote good practice through environmental management for medium and small businesses (Dimbleby, 569).

1986 *February.* Visits Texas and California—Charles suggested in a speech that developers should build on vacant land in the inner cities rather than push planners to open more land in the Green Belt.

September. Speech at Harvard (350th anniversary celebrations) and visit to Chicago.

The Youth Business Initiative is merged into the Prince's Youth Business Trust. Currently they have a volunteer network of fifty-five hundred advisers and a turnover from their business ventures of £1 million. It is a model for other initiatives in the U.S., Canada, and India. The government commits £10 million in matching grants with an equal amount being raised by the private sector to finance a three-year expansion scheme (Dimbleby, 568).

1987 *February.* Speaks at the European Year of the Environment where he says, "Why then are we so slow in this country to respond to what is, I think, a growing public feeling? Why has environmental regulation of one kind or another taken so long to come about here when you find that in Western Germany, for instance, or the United States, they have had many more regulations and controls for a long[er] time than we have?" He went on to say he had banned aerosol products in his house (Dimbleby, 425).

March. Visits NATO headquarters

March. Official visit to Swaziland, Malawi, and Kenya as director of the Commonwealth Development Corporation.

1988 *March.* United States—attends "Remaking the Cities" Conference, Pittsburgh. This conference was key for a number of reasons. It was the first time something like this had been done in the United States. The topics were urbanism, community architecture, and public-private partnerships. The conference was a joint effort between the American Institute of Architecture and the British Institute of Architecture.

At a European Environment Conference Charles says, "There is a growing realisation that we are not separate from Nature; a subconscious feeling that we need to restore a feeling of harmony with Nature and a proper sense of respect and awe for the great mystery of the natural order of the Universe. . . . We are beginning to realise that whatever we do to Nature—whether it is on the grandest scale or just in our own gardens—is ultimately something that we are doing to our own deepest selves" (holism).

1989 The prince forms a core group of environmental advisers around him, which includes Richard Sandbrook, executive director of the International Institute for Environment and Development; Jonathan Porritt, director of Friends of the Earth; and Janet Barber, head of conservation at the World Wildlife Fund U.K., now called Worldwide Fund for Nature. There were others who provided advice, such as Tim O'Riordan, professor of environmental sciences at the University of East Anglia, and Richard Aylard who, as the prince's aide, was a committed environmentalist.

"Business in the Environment, launched by the prince in 1989 is linked to some twenty-nine hundred companies and fifty environmental networks promoting good practice through environmental management publications for medium and small businesses. 'Opportunity 2000,' a campaign to increase the participation of women in the workplace, is supported by more than two hundred fifty employers, who between them represent twenty-five percent of the British workforce" (Dimbleby, 569).

Spring. At a speech before the "Saving the Ozone Layer" World Conference, Charles says: "Until we have managed to discover somewhere else in some other galaxy which has a comparable set of atmospheric conditions, it makes absolutely *no* sense to me at any rate to mess about unnecessarily with the fragile and delicate chemical composition which perpetuate life on this globe as it hurtles mysteriously and harmoniously through space. It certainly makes no sense to destroy the ozone layer" (Dimbley, 427–28). (The U.S. Senate will vote on climate warming in December 1997.)

1990 The first Prince of Wales Business Leaders Forum is held in Charleston, South Carolina. They have since held over twenty-six international forum meetings, which have involved four thousand business leaders in North America, Latin America, Europe, and Asia. In addition, Business Leaders forums have been established in Poland, the Czech Republic, Slovakia, St. Petersburg, India, and Mexico, to name a few places.

1990 The Prince sponsors an environmental film, *The Earth in Balance.*

At the recommendation of Maurice Strong, the secretary-general of the 1992 Rio Earth Summit, Swiss industrialist Stephen Schmidheiny brought together a group of forty-eight business leaders from twenty-five countries to present the global business perspective on the environment to the Rio conference. As a result of the 1992 conference, the World Industry Council for the Environment was established in 1995 (see 1995).

1991 Prince Charles does a "timely TV documentary on the environment which was the centerpiece of a European-wide campaign to raise public awareness about the future of the planet." Charles also visits an Indonesian rainforest as well as makes an historic visit to Hungary (*Royalty*, Jan. 1991, vol 10. no. 4).

April. Charles hosts a key meeting aboard the royal yacht to bring together key international figures in an attempt to achieve a degree of harmony between the conflicting attitudes of Europe, the U.S., and the developing nations with regard to the planned 1992 Rio summit. Among those invited were then-Senator Al Gore, senior officials from the World Bank, CEOs from Shell and BP, principal non-governmental organizations, European politicians, and the president of Brazil. According to some present, Charles also played a crucial role in preparing north and south for the accommodation in their positions, which would be needed for the Rio summit (Dimbleby, 497–98).

Charles, in a keynote address to the World Commission on Environment and Development (the Brundtland Commission), commends their findings: "There is little doubt that your Commission's report, in 1987, was the single most important document of the decade on this subject, bringing the phrase 'sustainable development' into all our vocabularies. Now, I happen to be a firm believer in the precautionary principle—recognizing that the systems which keep our Earth habitable are extremely complex and may operate in ways beyond human understanding. Commissioners, your chairman, speaking in Cambridge last year, argued with eloquence that a new triad should be recognized: environment plus development plus democracy. The challenge of Rio is to see how that triad can be put into effect. A first requirement will be a stronger commitment by one and all to create a balance, within nations, between nations and between generations" (*Population and Development Review* 18, no. 2, June 1992).

June. The International Partnership Network is formed to discuss the role of partnership work. Its goals are: (1) The advocacy of partnership approaches to sustainable development; (2) the encouragement of regional networks based on specific themes; and (3) the building of capacity.

The Institute of Architecture is founded by the prince to explore, teach, and promote ways of improving the quality of the built environment. Both a summer school and a two-year study course are available. The institute conducts summer classes in the United States as well as Europe.

International Hotel Environment Initiative is founded when the CEO of Inter-Continental Hotels approaches the Prince of Wales Business Leaders Forum with a new idea.

November. Members of the PWBLF arranged for Minister Qu Ge-ping to join the Prince of Wales in Hong Kong at meetings to discuss the part business can play in sustainable development. Companies represented included Coca-Cola, Coopers & Lybrand, Sedgwick China, DLH, Cable & Wireless, Wheelock, Shell China, and IBM China.

1993 Charles visits the United States of America and Mexico. In Mexico he expounds "his environmental message, which is rapidly becoming the focus of his life." He also chairs the final session of a meeting of his Business Leaders Forum. On his initiative, the business leaders, including over one hundred influential Mexican captains of industry, agree to launch a widespread program to bring fresh water supplies to poor rural communities. "Charles also brings to Mexico the idea of his Business in Community venture, well established in Britain, whereby business leaders agree to divert some of their profits to help local people in the areas where their factories are situated. We should expect to see and hear more of him as a major environmental figure on the world stage." In the United States, Charles arrives at William and Mary College to take part in the 300th anniversary celebrations. He also visits Vice-President and Mrs. Gore who host a small dinner party for him. He then meets President Clinton (*Majesty*, April 1993).

Poland Initiative—One hundred fifty entrepreneurs attend the MASTER class to gain insight from international business leaders

St. Petersburg Initiative through the PWBLF established

Prince Charles' Duchy of Cornwall becomes one of the most profitable and largest organic farms in the country. Currently Duchy Originals, organic biscuits made with oats from the prince's Highgrove estate, are exported all over Europe.

1994 In an interview with the BBC the prince says, "So much I try to do is behind the scenes. It is not done in the full glare of media attention. So it is difficult for people to understand how all the things fit together." He also asserts that there is a common theme to all his projects and insists they will turn out to be for the long term good.

The prince launches his new magazine on architecture called *Perspectives*. The sole investor in the magazine is the Prince of Wales Institute of Architecture (*Majesty*, May 1994). Charles says of his new endeavor, "We are told constantly that we must create the spirit of the age. What I am hoping for is an age which has spirit."

Charles speaks at the Worldwide Fund for Nature Timber seminar in London and stresses his "overwhelming sense of despair at the destruction of the world's forests." He stresses that the royal household will use only wood supplied from sustainable sources from 1995 (*Royalty*, vol. 12, no. 12).

The prince tours St. Petersburg where it is hoped his trip will create further Western investment in the city. It is hoped that his visit will be an attempt to reconcile the Anglo-Russian differences from the past. He attends a meeting of his Business Leaders Forum (*Royalty*, vol. 13, no. 1).

The prince visits Hungary where he meets with entrepreneurs at the Business Leaders Forum and where he inaugurates a new printing machine, installed due to British investment (*Royalty*, vol. 13, no. 1).

Partners for Growth is established by forty top business leaders to tackle unemployment. The main objective is to encourage the establishment of direct linkages between large-scale companies and small indigenous enterprises.

June. Charles explains his preference for ecumenicalism. "I've always felt that the Catholic subjects of the sovereign are equally important as the Anglican ones, as the

Protestant ones. Likewise I think that the Islamic subjects or the Hindu subjects or the Zoroastrian subjects of the sovereign are of equal and vital importance" (Dimbleby, 528).

In discussing the relationship of the sovereign to the Church of England, Charles says, with regard to the title of Defender of the Faith, that he would prefer it to be Defender of Faith (Dimbleby, 528).

The PWBLF launches a new project called "Inner-City Action," which links community leaders in the United States and other western countries to their counterparts in developing world countries to tackle jointly shared problems of youth unemployment, ethnic minority conflict, shortages of housing, and environmental degradation.

1995 AIESEC (the world's largest student-managed organization) and the Prince of Wales Business Leaders Forum embark on a joint initiative to answer questions of business

January. Charles tours Hong Kong and attends the British Chamber of Commerce there. Charles also spends five days in Hollywood meeting with his Business Leaders Forum on the need for partnership in troubled city communities. Charles toured gang-infested areas of Los Angeles.

March. National Business Initiative (BNI) for Growth, Development, and Democracy set up in South Africa. The goal is to support the creation of public-private partnerships. In 1995, the BNI formed a strategic alliance with the PWBLF.

May. The prince tours Northern Africa which includes Cairo, the Valley of the Kings, the Ibn Tulun Mosque, and the Greek Orthodox Monastery of St. Catherine in the Sinai desert. In Casablanca the prince addresses "Kingdoms in Partnership," the largest British trade fair ever staged on North African soil.

The prince addresses a conference on "Britain in the World" at the Royal Institute of International Affairs. Other speakers included Prime Minister John Major and former United States Secretary of State Henry Kissinger (*Majesty*, May 1995).

The Walt Disney Co. is to distribute the children's video *The Legend of Lochnagar* which is based on a story Charles wrote in 1970 to amuse his brothers in the U.S. and Canada. All profits will be passed on to the Prince's Trust.

The Prince of Wales's company, Duchy Originals, the commercial arm of the Duchy of Cornwall set up in 1990, launches an up-market range of nonalcoholic beverages. The drinks will be produced and marketed in conjunction with soft-drink giants Coca-Cola and British firm Cadbury Schwepps *(Majesty*, May 1995).

June. The Prince visits Canada for Hamilton's 150th anniversary celebrations

1996 *July.* Community Action—India Business and Community Partnership bring senior figures together from major Indian investors

July. The World Bank hosts its first major meeting on

corporate citizenship in September 1996. In July the prince meets the president of the World Bank. PWBLF members and partners take a leading role with four hundred fifty participants from industrialized and developing countries. Sir David Simon of British Petroleum and Percey Barnevik of ABB speak.

The World Industry Council for the Environment and the Charter for Sustainable Development merges to set up the World Business Council for Sustainable Development, which is a coalition of more than one hundred twenty business leaders drawn from over thirty-four countries and twenty major industrial sectors. In 1995 it produced a report with the cooperation with the Prince of Wales Business Leaders Forum that led to the establishment of a leadership development program. In partnership with the United Nations Environmental Program and *Greencross International,* the World Business Council for Sustainable Development is working on a program to transfer expertise on environmental emergency response to central and eastern Europe. (It should be noted that Mikhail Gorbachev is president and founder of *Greencross International.)*

September. The prince visits North Carolina where the first American summer school sponsored by the Prince of Wale's Institute of Architecture was being held.

October. PWBFL and the Hungarian Business Leaders Forum sponsor, "Skills for Tomorrow: Investing in People," in Budapest

November. PWBFL trains one hundred fifty entrepreneurs

December. Windsor Castle Roundtable on Social and Ethical Accounting and Auditing is hosted by the New Economics Foundation, the Institute of Social and Ethical Accountability, and SustainAbility Ltd.

Note: The above is not a total representation of the meetings, speeches, and appointments of Prince Charles, but is provided as a small sampling of some of his activities and his deep involvement in the global governmental and environmental affairs of this world. In many cases, the month in which an activity occurred was not provided and therefore is left blank.

Other Sources:

Royalty
Vol. 13, No. 6, January 1995
Vol. 12, No. 12
Vol. 13, No. 11
Vol. 10, No. 4, January 1991
Vol. 14, No. 4, April 1993

Majesty
Vol. 15, No. 1
Vol. 16, No. 5, May 1995
Vol. 15, No. 5, May 1994
Vol. 15, No. 12, Dec. 1994
Vol. 17, No. 6, June 1996
Vol. 14, No. 4, April 1993

Appendix G

Comparison—
Charles, Prince of Wales to
Jesus Christ, Prince of Peace

Charles, Prince of Wales	Jesus Christ, Redeemer of the World
• Born at Buckingham Palace with great fanfare and celebration	• Virgin born in a stable—angels heralded the birth of the Savior of the World
• Parents are rulers of this world as queen and prince of Great Britain and the Commonwealth	• Earthly parents were poor people of lineage to King David who had no earthly aristocratic standing
• The heritage of the British royal family can be traced to the eighth century. The lineage of Charles can be traced to the titular kings of Jerusalem back to Babylon. Charles is Jewish by his father's father.	• Jesus was before the foundations of this world and at the creation. He is the Great I AM. Born in the City of David, the Messiah is Jewish.

- The Queen rides in a gold carriage, and Charles in limousines, Rolls Royces, and sports cars.

- Jesus walked, as He had no conveyance.

- The royal family has hundreds of servants who wait on their every desire and need.

- Jesus washed the feet of his disciples and said, "If I then, your Lord and Master, have washed your feet; ye also ought to wash one another's feet" (John 13:14).

- Charles went to private schools and graduated from Oxford University.

- Jesus apparently had no formal education.

- In 1958, when Charles was almost 10 years of age, the queen bestowed upon him the title of Prince of Wales to be invested at age 21.

- When Jesus was 12 years of age, he spent three days in the synagogue asking questions of the doctors and learned rabbis.

- Invested at Caernarvon Castle and given all of the symbols of kingship (robe, crown, sword, scepter), presented at the north, south, east, and west sides of the castle.

- The only crown and robe Jesus received was the crown of thorns in mockery. Soldiers cast dice for the robe.

- Trained as a naval officer, earning wings as he learned to fly a helicopter and a number of sophisticated jet fighters. Charles is a military leader.

- A teacher, Jesus lived in territory occupied by Rome. He came to set men at variance with one another—father with son, mother and daughter.

- In a quest for inner meaning, Charles turned to nature—Gaia—the worship of earth. He believes in the virtues of each religion, but discounts Jesus Christ.

- Married a virgin to produce heirs while he was having an affair with a married woman. It was this adulterous relationship which broke up his marriage.

- A Renaissance man—action, sports, music, theater, drama, art

- Has set up a number of trusts to help the poor; all profits go to his trust.

- A businessman, Charles spearheads the Prince of Wales Business Leaders Forum, working with the world's leading multinational corporations on environmental issues.

- Charles is active on the global level, behind the scenes. He

- It is through the blood of Jesus Christ that man has forgiveness of sins and is saved eternally. We worship the Creator, not the creation.

- The Son of God knew no women and He honored them, as it was Mary Magdalene to whom He showed Himself after He rose from the grave.

- Jesus—the One who created the seasons, music, art—said: "I am the Way, the Truth, and the Life. . . ."

- Ministered to the poor—preaching, healing, teaching. The rich have no need of a doctor.

- The businessmen, leading learned officials, and soldiers came to Jesus seeking His counsel, healing, and words of life.

- The whole mission of Jesus Christ was to redeem man's

works in secret, bringing together key players through the global governmental body, the United Nations. He has guided the U.N. radical environmental agenda, which will change how the world lives— an agenda that will lead to bondage.

■ Charles meets regularly with world leaders when he visits their countries.

■ Today people say, "God save the Queen," as a tribute to the monarch.

■ Charles, in his Business Leaders Forum, concentrates on the developing countries of the East.

■ Charles has been a critic of modern architecture, preferring classical architecture. His Institute of Architecture concentrates on the holism of buildings and their interaction with their surroundings and nature.

■ Wherever the prince goes he has many, many followers and

fallen state through His sacrifice on the cross and provide forgiveness of sin and eternal life. Jesus provides hope to the downtrodden and freedom for all who believe in Him. All that Jesus did was in the open. There was nothing that he did in secret.

■ The only world leader Jesus met was Pontius Pilate.

■ In Jesus' day they cried, "Hosanna," meaning "save," or "help now."

■ The gospel of Jesus Christ began in the Middle East.

■ Although Jesus was a carpenter, the Greek word is used in contempt, as Jesus is the great Architect, Designer, and Fabricator of all material creations and of all moral creations (*Dake's Bible*, 259).

■ Jesus is the name above all names. At His Second Com-

admirers. He is watched and tracked by many in the world.

- Charles is the uncrowned (future) king of England.

- The symbol for the British royal family is the red dragon.

- Charles, the Sustainable Prince.

ing, all men will bow their knees to Him.

- Jesus is the uncrowned King of Kings.

- Jesus came as the Lamb of God.

- Jesus, the Everlasting Prince!

Appendix H

Rhodes Confession of Faith

As taken from Lord Milner's papers at Oxford University
located at Mss. Afr.tr. #17
and copied from a copy located in the
Rhodes archives at Georgetown University
copy courtesy of Dr. Stanley Monteith

It often strikes a man to enquire what is the chief good in life; to one the thought comes that it is a happy marriage, to another great wealth, and as each seizes on his idea, for that he more or less works for the rest of his existence. To myself thinking over the same question the wish came to render myself useful to my country. I then asked myself how could I and after reviewing the various methods I have felt that at the present day we are actually limiting our children and perhaps bringing into the world half the human beings we might owing to the lack of country for them to inhabit that if we had retained America there would at the present moment be millions more of English living. I contend that we are the finest race in the world and that the more of the world we inhabit the better it is for the human race. Just fancy those parts that are at present inhabited by the most despicable specimen of human beings what all alteration there would be if they were brought under Anglo-Saxon influence, look again at the extra employment a new country added to our dominions gives. I contend that every acre added to our territory means in the future birth to some more of the English race who otherwise would not be brought into existence. Added to this the absorption of the greater portion of the world under our rule simply means the end of all wars, at this moment had we not lost America I believe we could have stopped the present Russo-Turkish war by merely refusing money and supplies. Having these ideas what scheme could we think of to forward this object. I look into history and I read the story of the Jesuits I see what they were able to do in a bad cause and I might say under bad leaders.

In the present day I become a member in the Masonic order I see the wealth and power they possess the influence they hold and I think over their ceremonies and I wonder that a large body of men can devote themselves to what at times appears the most ridiculous and absurd rites without an object and without an end.

The idea gleaming and dancing before ones eyes like a will-of-the-wisp at last frames itself into a plan. Why should we not form a secret society with but one object the furtherance of the British Empire and the bringing of the whole uncivilized world under British rule for the recovery of the United States for the making the Anglo-Saxon race but one Empire. What a dream, but yet it is probable. It is possible. I once heard it argued by a fellow in my own college, I am sorry to own it by an Englishman, that it was a good thing for us that we have lost the United States. There are some subjects on which there can be no arguments, and to an Englishman this is one of them, but even from an American point of view just picture what they have lost, look at their Government, are not the frauds that yearly come before the public view a disgrace to any country and especially theirs which is the finest in the world. Would they have occurred if they had remained under English rule great as they have become how infinitely greater they would have been with the softening and elevating influences of English rule, think of those countless thousands of Englishmen that during the last hundred years would have crossed the Atlantic and settled and populated the United States. Would they have not made without any prejudice a finer country of it than the low class Irish and German emigrants? All this we have lost and that country loses owing to whom? Owing to two or three ignorant pig-headed statesmen in the last century, at their door lies the blame. Do you ever feel mad? Do you ever feel murderous? I think I do with those men. I bring facts to prove my assertion. Does an English father when his sons wish to emigrate ever think of suggesting emigration to a country under another flag, never—it would seem a disgrace to suggest such a thing, I think that we all think that poverty is better under our own flag than wealth under a foreign one.

Put your mind into another train of thought. Fancy Australia discovered and colonized under the French flag, what would it mean merely several millions of English unborn that at present exist. We learn from the past to form our future. We learn from having lost to cling to what we possess. We know the size of the world we know now the total extent. Africa is still lying ready for us it is our duty to take it. It is our duty to seize every opportunity of acquiring more territory and we should keep this one idea steadily before our eyes that more territory simply means more of the Anglo-Saxon race more of the best most human, most honourable race the world possesses.

To forward such a scheme what a splendid help a secret society would be a society not openly acknowledged but who would work in secret for such an object.

I contend that there are at the present moment numbers of the ablest men in the world who would devote their whole lives to it. I often think what a loss to the English nation in some respects the abolition of the rotten Borough system has been. What thought strikes a man entering the House of Commons, the Assembly that rules the whole World? I think it is the mediocrity of the men but what is the cause? It is simply an assembly of wealth of men whose lives have been spent in the accumulation of money whose time has been too much engaged to be able to spare any for the study of past history. And yet in the hands of such men rest our destinies. Do men like the great Pitt and Burke and Sheridan not now exist? I contend they do. There are men now living with I know no other term the megcloyucod of Aristotle but there are no ways for enabling them to serve their Country. They live and die unused unemployed. What has been the main cause of the success of the Romish Church? The fact that every enthusiast, call it if you like every madman, finds employment in it. Let us form the same kind of society a Church for the extension of the British Empire, a society which should have its members in every part of the British Empire working with one object and one idea who should have its members placed at every University and our schools and should watch the English youth passing through their hands just one perhaps in every thousand would have the mind and feelings for such an object, he should be tried in every way, he should be tested whether he is endurant, possessed of eloquence, disregardful of the petty details of life and if found to be such then elected and bound by oath to serve for the rest of his life his Country. He should then be supported if without means by the society and sent to that part of the Empire where it is felt he was needed.

Take another case, let us fancy a man finds himself his own master with ample means attaining his majority whether he puts the question directly to himself or not still like the old story of virtue and vice in the memorabilia a fight goes on in him as to what he shall do. Take it he plunges into dissipation there is nothing too reckless he does not attempt but after a time his life palls on him, he mentally says this is not good enough, he changes his life, he reforms, he travels, he thinks now I have found the chief good in life, the novelty wears off, and he tires, to change again, he goes into the far interior after the wild game he thinks at last I have found that in life of which I cannot tire, again he is disappointed. He returns he thinks is there nothing I can do in life? Here I am with means with good health with everything that is to be envied and yet I am not happy I am tired of life he possesses within him every portion of the Megdgoyocod of Aristotle but he knows it not, to such a man the Society should go, should test, and should finally show him the greatness of the scheme and list him as a member.

Take one more case of the younger son with high thoughts, high aspirations endowed by nature with all the faculties to make a great man, and with the sole wish in life to serve his Country but he lacks two things the means and the opportunity, ever troubled with a sort of inward deity urging him on to high and noble deeds, he is compelled to pass his time in some occupation which furnishes him with mere existence he lives unhappily and dies miserably. Such men as these the Society should search out and use for the furtherance of their object.

In every Colonial legislature the Society should attempt to have its members prepared at all times to vote for, speak, and advocate, the closer union of England and the Colonies to crush all disloyalty every movement for the severance of our Empire. The Society should inspire and even own portions of the press for the press rules the mind of the people. The society should always be searching for members who might by their position in the world by their energies or character forward its object but the ballot and test for admittance should be severe. Once make it common and it fails. Take a man of great wealth who is bereft of his children perhaps having his mind soured by some bitter disappointment, who shuts himself up separate from his neighbours and makes up his mind to a miserable existence. To such men as these the Society should go gradually disclose the greatness of their scheme and entreat him to throw in his life and property with them for this object. I think that there are thousands now existing who would eagerly grasp at the opportunity. Such are the heads of my scheme. For fear that death might cut me off before the time for attempting its development I leave all my worldly goods in trust to S. G. Shippard and the Secretary for the Colonies at the time of my death to try to form such an object.

Notes

1. John Major, *United Nations-UK New World* (October–December 1995): Special Insert [speech].
2. Robert I. Rotberg, *The Founder: Cecil Rhodes and the Pursuit of Power* (New York: Oxford University Press, 1988).
3. Ibid., 100.
4. Ibid., 102.
5. Carroll Quigley, *The Anglo-American Establishment* (New York: Books in Focus, 1981), ix.
6. Ibid., ix.
7. Ibid., 7.
8. Ibid., 34.
9. Ibid., 5.
10. Ibid., 137.
11. William L. Tung, *International Organization Under the United Nations System* (New York: Thomas Crowell Company, 1969), 87.
12. Basil Blackwell, *The First Fifty Years of the Rhodes Trust and the Rhodes Scholarships* (Oxford: A. R. Mowbray & Company Ltd., 1955), 233–234.
13. Ibid., 211.
14. Ibid., 211–213
15. Prince Philip, HRH Duke of Edinburgh, British Embassy, *Washington Times*, 9 June 1997, c12.
16. Dennis Cuddy, *Secret Records Revealed*, (Marlborough: The Plymouth Rock Foundation, 1995), 3.
17. *The Washington Times*, "New World Order Confusion," 16

October 1991.

18. Prince Charles, "The Prince of Wales on Population and the Environment," *Population and Development Review* 18 (June 1992), 384.

19. Anthony Holden, *King Charles III* (New York: Weidenfeld & Nicholson, 1988), 116.

20. Anthony Holden, *Charles, Prince of Wales* (London: Weidenfeld & Nicholson, 1979), 284.

21. Gerald Paget, *The Lineage and Ancestry of H.R.H. Prince Charles, Prince of Wales,* vol. 1 (Baltimore: Genealogical Publishing Co., Inc., 1977), ix.

22. Paget, vol. 2, 494.

23. Holden, *King Charles III,* 225–26.

24. Holden, *Charles, Prince of Wales,* App. F.

25. Jonathan Dimbleby, *The Prince of Wales: A Biography* (New York: William Morrow & Company, 1994), 428–29.

26. Ibid., 247.

27. Ibid., 251.

28. Ibid., 255.

29. Holden, *King Charles III,* 145.

30. Frank V. Cahouet, *Remaking the Cities, Proceedings of the 1988 International Conference in Pittsburgh,* ed. Barbara Davis (Pittsburgh Chapter of the American Institute of Architects, 1989), 45–47.

31. U.S. MAB Bulletin, Vol. 20, No. 2, (Washington, D.C.: Department of State), July 1997, 2.

32. Donella H. and Denis L. Meadows, Jorgen Randers, and William W. Behrens III, *Limits to Growth* (New York: Universe Books, 1973), 9.

33. Ibid., 25.

34. Ibid., 21.

35. Ibid., 23.

36. Ibid., 66.

37. Ibid., 170.

38. Dimbleby, *Prince of Wales*, 423.
39. Ibid., 497.
40. Armand Hammer with Neil Lyndon, *Hammer* (New York: G.P. Putnam's Sons, 1987), 394. (All proceeds from his book went to the United World Colleges.)
41. Ibid, 511.
42. Ibid, 512.
43. Frank Barnaby, gen. ed., *The Gaia Peace Atlas* (New York: Gaia Book Limited and Doubleday, 1988), 223.
44. Steven Weinberg, *Armand Hammer: The Untold Story* (Boston: Little, Brown and Company, 1989), 22.
45. United Nations General Assembly 38th Session, "Resolutions and Decisions adopted by the General Assembly during its Thirty-Eighth Session," 20 September–20 December 1983, and 26 June 1984, 129. (A/38/47).
46. International Union for Conservation of Nature and Natural Resources, *World Conservation Strategy* (Switzerland: International Union for Conservation of Nature and Natural Resources, 1980), cover.
47. Ibid., p.1.
48. United Nations General Assembly, 38/161, 131.
49. The World Commission on Environment and Development, *Our Common Future* (New York, Oxford University Press, 1987), 353–356.
50. Ibid., 366–387.
51. Ibid., 43.
52. Jacqueline Kasun, *The WAR against Population* (San Francisco: Ignatius Press, 1988).
53. International Planned Parenthood Federation, *Vision 2000 and the ICPD Programme of Action*, (London: Regent's College, 1995).
54. S. E. Finer, ed. *Five Constitutions: Contrasts and Comparison* (Middlesex: Penguin Books, 1979), 153.
55. Jane Nelson, *Business as Partners in Development,* (London:

PWBLF, 1996) 2.

56. The Commission on the Status of Women, 39th Session, "Proposals for Consideration in the Preparation of a Draft Declaration and the Draft Platform for Action, the Advanced Unedited Version Future A/Conf. 177/L.1" (15 May 1995) 14, no. 32.

57. Ibid., Jane Nelson, 50.

58. United Nations Development Programme, "Governance for Sustainable Human Development," (January 1997), iv.

59. Speech by Carolyn McAskie for Huguette Labelle, President of the Canadian International Development Agency (who could not attend). Panel: "The Global Treaties: Making Connections for Efficiencies, Effectiveness, and Equity" (Fifth Annual World Bank Conference on Environmentally and Socially Sustainable Development, 6-6-11 October 1997, Washington, D.C.)

60. Bill Clinton, "A New Spirit . . . for a New Century." *The Washington Post*, 21 January 1997, a.

61. United Nations Development Programme, "Governance for Sustainable Human Development," (January 1997), i.

62. Ibid., 14.

63. The Commission on Global Governance, *Our Global Neighborhood* (New York: Oxford University Press, 1995), 251.

64. Erskine Childers with Brian Urquhart, *Renewing the United Naitons System*, (Uppsala, Sweden: Dag Hammarskjold Foundation, 1994), 176.

65. Barnaby, *The Gaia Peace Atlas*, 239.

66. Parliamentarians for Global Action, *Reviving the Global Economy* [brochure] and *Annual Report*, 1994.

67. World Economic Forum, *Annual Reports* 1995–96, 1997.

68. Erica Carl, "The Chamber of Commerce—Its Power and Goals," December, 1983.

69. World Business Council for Sustainable Development, *Annual Review* 1996.

70. The Commission on Global Governance, 266.

71. Ron Arnold and Alan Gottlieb, Trashing the Economy (Bellevue: Enterprise Press, 1994), 537–538.

72. Ibid., 81ff.

73. Bertram Gross, Friendly Fascism, (Boston: South End Press, 1980), 11.

74. Ibid., 28.

75. *Wisconsin Reports*, Multilateral Agreement on Investment," 14 August 97, 2–3.

76. William Ebenstein, *Today's isms: Communism, Fascism, Capitalism, Socialism,* (Englewood Cliffs: Prentice-Hall, Inc., 1972), 67.

77. Prince of Wales Business Leaders Forum, "Stakeholders: The Challenge in a Global Market, Conclusions and Follow-up Action" (Charleston, South Carolina, 20–21 February, 1990), 5–6.

78. Ibid., 6.

79. Ibid., 7.

80. Prince of Wales Business Leaders Forum 1990-1995 Report, London: (Prince of Wales Business Leaders Forum), 4.

81. Grand Metropolitan, *Your Environment . . . We Value It* [corporate brochure]

82. Ibid.

83. Ibid.

84. Grand Metropolitan Community Relations, *Report on Corporate Citizenship 1997*, (Brighton, England, 1997), 27–32.

85. Jane Nelson, *Business as Partners in Development—Creating wealth for countries, companies and communities*, 52.

86. Compilation by writer of numerous activities and projects as portrayed in numerous publications by the Prince of Wales Business Leaders Forum.

87. Telephone interview with James Newsome, spokesman for the Prince of Wales Business Leaders Forum (London, September 9, 1997).

88. AIESEC, "Educating Tomorrow's Global Business Leaders," London: (Prince of Wales Business Leaders Forum, London), 31.
89. Ibid., 40.
90. *Majesty*, May 1994, 10.
91. Interview with Donald Lehr, 19 October 1997, and press release, no date, entitled "The Templeton Prize: Acknowledging Progress in Religion." (Donald Lehr is the Public Affairs Director with the Nolan/Lehr Group in New York for the Templeton Prize.)
92. Templeton Award for Progress in Religion Press kit. (The Nolan/Lehr Group, New York.)
93. Prince of Wales Business Leaders Forum, "Challenge and Change 1992–2000" (London: International Hotels Environment Initiative), 11.
94. Ibid, Intro.

Synopsis

Prince Charles the Sustainable Prince
Paragraphs of Key Importance

Introduction

Our look cannot only deal with the man, but must deal with his politics which demand both an empowered U.N. and empowered multinational corporations. The politics of the prince, specifically his environmental philosophy, are enshrouded in "sustainable development" which is a merger between communism and capitalism. This merger then necessitates a new form of governance through public-private partnerships. The picture is complete when one considers both the empowered United Nations (which the royal family directs), and the empowered multinational corporations (which Charles influences through the Prince of Wales Business Leaders Forum).When all of these are placed into operation through public-private partnerships, all of society, as we know it, will change. We must understand each of these things in order to know the "day and hour."

Chapter One
The Rhodes Legacy

Of particular interest with regard to the Milner (Kindergarten) Group was how the world would be ruled once under the British Empire. According to Quigley:

> They feared the British Empire might fall into the same

difficulty and destroy British idealism and British liberties by
the tyranny necessary to hold on to a reluctant Empire. And
any effort to hold an empire by tyranny they regarded as doomed
to failure. . . . The Group feared that all culture and civilization
would go down to destruction because of our inability to construct some kind of political unit larger than the national state,
just as Greek Culture and civilization in the fourth century B.C.
went down to destruction because of the Greeks' inability to
construct some kind of political unit larger than the city-state.
This was the fear that had animated Rhodes, and it was the
same fear that was driving the Milner Group to transform the
British Empire into a Commonwealth of Nations and then place
that system within a League of Nations.[10]

The United Nations became the successor to the League of
Nations in 1945. While there are a number of major differences between the two organizations, the biggest difference
was an empowered U.N. The decisions of the League [of Na-
tions] Council were essentially recommendations, whereas "the
decisions of the [United Nations] Security Council are legally
binding upon the Members of the United Nations"[11]

Chapter Three
Philosophical Components of the Agenda
Public-Private Partnerships. What is "public-private partnership"? Public-private partnership is just what it says it is.
First, it is a business arrangement, sealed by an agreement or,
in some cases, a handshake. The terms of the partnership will
vary according to partners and objectives. Second, the parties
in the partnership are public and private entities. Public entities refer to government—local, county, state, federal, and/or
global agencies. Private refers to nongovernmental groups such
as foundations, nonprofit groups, corporations, and individuals. For example, foundations could include the Ford,

Rockefeller, or the local "good-works" foundation; nonprofits could refer to nongovernmental organizations like the Prince of Wales Business Leaders Forum, the Nature Conservancy, the Sierra Club, World Wildlife Federation, Planned Parenthood, or NOW; and corporations could be any corporation from a small one, to a multinational like Exxon, Johnson Wax, 3M, Black and Decker, or Giant Foods. Lastly, individuals could be any person—such as a businessman, rancher, or dentist.

A public-private partnership will always have as its goal a business-making venture that requires some form of "governance." The question is, since the players will vary in experience and wealth, who has the most power? We know from life itself that whoever has the most money has the power. For example, when a public-private partnership is comprised of governments such as the County Department of Environmental Initiatives, the State Department of Environmental Resources; a number of private entities like a land trust (foundation) and the Nature Conservancy (nonprofit); along with a corporation such as Black and Decker, the players with the most money contol the partnership. In this case, it would be the Nature Conservancy, with assets of over $1 billion and Black and Decker Corporation, with a capitalization of $1.6 billion. Representative government loses.

Public-private partnerships were "unveiled" in June 1996 at the United Nations Conference on Human Settlements, Habitat II, held in Istanbul. It took me nine months of research from the Habitat II conference to understand what a public-private partnership was. The document which finally helped me to understand its importance and implications was from the *U.S. Man and Biosphere Bulletin* which said:

> The long term goals of the U.S. MAB Program is to contribute to achieving a sustainable society early in the twenty-first century. The MAB mission and long term goal will be im-

plemented, in the United States and internationally, through public-private partnerships and linkages that sponsor and promote cooperative, interdisciplinary research, experimentation, education and information exchange on options by which societies can achieve sustainability. (Adopted by the U.S. National committee for the Man and the Biosphere Program, July 26, 1995.)[31]

In an interview I conducted with Dr. Wally N'Dow, secretary-general of the Habitat II conference, he said:

We have gotten to a point where we cannot not partner with the private sector, as governments, as the civil society, as NGO's, but also as people active in international development such as the United Nations. That is what Istanbul tried to convey.

In a follow-up interview with Dr. Noel Brown, former director of the United Nations Environment Programme and current special advisor to the Group of 77, he said of public-private partnerships:

I believe that the future of the U.N. will rest on effective partnering with the private sector—with business and industry. But I also believe that the environment and the environmental community must also rethink its mission and redefine its role as we enter the phase of globalization and as we are on the threshold of the 21st century.

In addition to revitalizing Pittsburgh, public-private partnerships have been used for the last twenty years in America as a method of providing financing to low-income families. HUD and its Office of Community Planning and Development has used public-private partnerships to create affordable housing since 1990. In addition, Maryland, Oregon, and Minnesota have implemented state-level public-private partnerships. It should be noted that as public-private partnerships continue to rise in the U.S., our Constitution and private property rights are being eroded.

Gaia—The Philosophical Shift. As mentioned, the first United Nations environmental conference was held in 1972 with the second one, the United Nations Conference on the Environment and Development (UNCED), held twenty years later. UNCED, also called the Earth Summit, was an unveiling of the philosophical shift from the Judeo-Christian world view to Gaia. The Programme of Action, called *Agenda 21*, is 297 pages long, and a second related document, *Global Biodiversity Assessment*, is over 1,100 pages long. Together these documents contain an agenda that can only be called evil, as the implementation of the action items will turn freedom into bondage and life into misery as all of what we know today will be replaced with a planned electronic society in which our only value will be to produce. This is the agenda Prince Charles is facilitating. In feudalistic times only the king and nobility owned land and had freedom. So, too, under United Nations rule, feudalistic times will return and the lights of freedom will go out. Charles has nothing to lose and the world to gain.

Chapter Four
Sustainable Development

Let me provide for you my own paraphrased definition of sustainable develpment, which I think is simpler to understand and embraces all of their points: The world has too many people, and if we do not reduce the number of people on planet Earth, they will use up all of the earth's resources so that future generations will be left without any resources. The United Nations is the best global body to monitor and manage and preserve the resources of the planet.

The Philosophy of Sustainable Development. Where does this concept come from? Before I went to the June 1996 United Nations Conference on Human Settlements (Habitat II) in Istanbul, I was trying to figure out just where sustainable development came from. The number of people serving on the World Commission on Environment and Development who were communist, Marxist or socialist provided my first clue. In thinking about that, it occurred to me that this philosophy is not in our Constitution. I then looked in a constitution opposite of ours, the constitution of the Union of Soviet Socialist Republics (1977). I found my answer in Chapter 2, Article 18, which states:

> In the interests of the present and future generations, the necessary steps are taken in the USSR to protect and make scientific, rational use of the land and its mineral and water resources, and the plant and animal kingdoms to preserve the purity of air and water, ensure reproduction of natural wealth, and improve the human environment.[54]

In the executive summary of the book *Business as Partners in Development: Creating Wealth for Countries, Companies and Communities,* the authors write:

> In most cases, the debate is no longer about extreme alternatives—about communism versus capitalism, the free market versus state control, democracy versus dictatorship—but about finding common good.[55]

The Result of Sustainable Development. This same intercon-nectedness can be seen in the merging of environment, economics and social issues into one. This is another aspect of the public-private partnership concept. As the environmental ideology permeates all aspects of life, it takes on a spiritual dimension that mirrors the Gaia philosophy, which is paganism. When the three become one through partnership, they form a philosophical approach that will change representative government in America. As the precepts of the Constitution are eliminated through new (United Nations policy-guided) legislation, the power of the Constitution is eroded, and in its place are public-private partnerships, which run parallel to representative government and form the new governance for the twenty-first century. This is a new twist to the concept of world government that most people visualize, and is the key to understanding how important is the Prince of Wales and the corporations to which he is providing leadership.

Chapter Five
Public-Private Partnerships and Governance Are ONE

It is on the global level that a number of key concepts and philosophies come together. Charles has adopted a very radical environmental agenda that calls for a planned society, using the environment and sustainable development as the reason for the change in governance (government) and freedoms. Public-private partnerships are the modus operandi to effect this change. The definition of governance by the UNDP is that public-private partnerships and governance (government) are one. In other words, sustainable development equals governance equals public-private partnerships equals ONE (government). We will be controlled on the local from the global, through public-private partnerships, bypassing the federal and state levels, rendering them obsolete.

James Gustave Speth said:

Just as important, we look forward to a *growing role in sup-*

*porting the involvement and participation of NGOs and civil
society organizations, including private business, in forging
partnerships of many types—partnerships [public-private]
that are an integral part of the web of global governance and
the glue that holds our troubled world together.*

Chapter Six
The Empowerment of the United Nations

In order to understand the power which Charles has, we must
look at the increased strength of both the United Nations and
transnational corporations. It is not enough to state "Charles
is powerful," one must explain how he is powerful in order to
understand the magnititude of the day and the hour. Not only
is the Rhodes legacy complete through the United Nations,
but the apex of the global governmental structure is being revealed through his actions and activities.

The Global (U.N.) to the Local Connection. Baltimore
mayor Kurt Schmoke, a Rhodes Scholar, was on the presidential delegation along with two other mayors from the United
States. I asked him what his presence meant. He replied in
part:

> Well, what I have tried to do here is to let other members
> of the delegation and those from around the world know how
> important this conference is to mayors in the United States.
> We just wanted people to know how important this conference
> is. It is the beginning of a new era with local government offi-
> cials being listened to in the development of U.N. documents
> and we see this as kind of the wave of the future.

Just as local chamber of commerce chapters receive direction
from the International Chamber of Commerce, so too, are
mayors receiving direction from the global U.N. level.

Multinational Corporations. The following is a message from Dr. David C. Korten. The following are excerpts from his Internet message:

> On June 24, 1997, the CEOs of ten TNCs [transnational corporations] met over lunch at the United Nations with the United Nations leadership and a number of senior government officials to chart a formalization of corporate involvement in the affairs of the United Nations. I attended the lunch. I found it a shattering experience for it revealed a seamless alliance between the public and private sectors aligned behind the consolidation of corporate rule over the global economy. . . .

Chapter Seven
Fascism and the Empowerment of Corporations

Many multinational and transnational corporations have assets and sales in excess of the value of most small and mid-size countries. As if this power were not enough, the Organization for Economic Cooperation and Development (OECD) in Paris is lobbying to pass the Multilateral Agreement on Investments (MAI), which would give corporations unlimited rights in any country that signs the agreement. In the words of Tony Clarke, director of the Polaris Institute in Canada:

> The MAI is designed to establish a whole new set of global rules for investments that will grant transnational corporations the unrestricted "right" and "freedom" to buy, sell, and move their operations whenever and wherever they want around the world, unfettered by government intervention or regulation. In short the MAI seeks to empower transnational corporations . . . by restrict[ing] . . . what national governments can and cannot do.[75]

I think the best definition of fascism, which basically points to everything the Prince of Wales believes and is doing, is:

Fascism adheres to the "philosopher-king" belief that only one class—which is by birth, education, or social standing —is capable of understanding what is best for the whole community and of putting it into practice.[76]

Chapter Eight
The Prince of Wales Business Leaders Forum

The Prince of Wales Business Leaders Forum is an educational charity with close to fifty multinational corporations from the United States, Britain, Germany, Japan, and several other countries, on its executive directorate. The United States corporations who work very closely with the prince include 3M, American Express, TRW, Coca-Cola, SmithKline Beecham, ARCO, CIGNA, DHL Worldwide Express, Levi Strauss & Company, the Perot Group, and U.S. WEST International. Additional partners are the American Chamber of Commerce, American Hotel & Motel Association, the Atlanta Project, Charles Stewart Mott Foundation, the City of Charleston, the Ford Foundation, the Kellogg Foundation, Eli Lilly, the New York City Housing Partnership, the Office of Ronald Reagan, the Soros Foundation, Texaco, Tufts University, Turner Broadcasting, USAID, and Warnaco, to name a few. The forum is accountable to a board and council made up of the international CEOs and directors from the above listed principal supporters and funded by its members with programs funded by other sponsors, international development agencies, and foundations. It works with the World Bank group, United Nations agencies, the European Commission, overseas development agencies, and a number of bilateral agencies from the U.K., Japan, and North America.

The mission of the Prince of Wales Business Leaders Forum is to promote continuous improvement in the practice of good *corporate citizenship* and *sustainable development internationally*, as a natural part of *successful business operations*. It aims to work with members and partners to:

1. Demonstrate that business has an essential and creative role to play in the prosperity of local communities as partners in development, particularly in economies in transition;
2. Raise awareness of the value of corporate responsibility in international business practice;
3. Encourage partnership action between business and communities as an effective means of promoting sustainable economic development.[81]

The Prince of Wales Business Leaders Forum operates in twenty-six countries, concentrating on post-communist countries and developing economies. They have held twenty-six high-level international meetings in eighteen countries involving five thousand corporate, government, and nongovernmental leaders.

Chapter Nine
Charles—The Hidden Prince

In an interview that Prince Charles gave on BBC's "Newsnight" program in 1994, he expressed his devotion to his work for Britain and the Commonwealth. He said, "so much I try to do is behind the scenes. So it is difficult for people to understand how all the things fit together." He also asserted that there is a common theme to all his projects and insisted they will turn out to be for the long term good.[85]

Charles—The Defender of Faith. As a result of my personal study, and in light of the above, I have come to believe that when the United States ratified the United Nations charter, we and the other countries of the world who were not part of Britain's Commonwealth, reverted back under British rule through the United Nations organizational structure. Therefore the fulfillment of the Rhodes Trust is complete.

King Charles III. There has been much speculation with regard as to when Charles will become king. I surmise that he does not need a throne, for he already has one. The environmental agenda via sustainable development, and public–private partnerships with the world's largest and strongest multinational corporations, many of which have cash flows and assets exceeding that of most countries, provide Charles his throne. It appears that he rules behind the scenes, encouraging, expanding, and pushing the agenda of the United Nations, partnering with the World Bank and other global agencies, all of which are advancing world government, a philosophy with which he is not uncomfortable. After all, there have been many kings, popes, and world leaders who have tried to attain it.

Conclusion

Because of who he is, doors automatically open and people flock to him. His tentacles are very long, reaching into every area of life, business, and government. He transcends politics, national borders, and religion. He is very powerful by way of position, lineage, inheritance, importance, and influence. He is out to remake society and mold it into his image, which is based on Gaia and corporate global governance through public-private partnerships. This will change life for every person on earth as we will become slaves to the new twenty-first century feudal landlords—those with the power and money. Sustainable development demands that every crust of bread eaten be measured against what a person produces in order to protect resources for future generations. Is all of this the new divine right of kings? Do you not realize the second American Revolution is in the process of being fought? The battle this time is philosophical, no guns or bullets. It is spiritual warfare at its finest. The person the mainstream media would have us believe Charles is—is not the real Charles. The real Charles has a global agenda of his own. He should be recognized as a *very major player* in the end-time game. What is your response?

Action

I believe that if this book has done anything, it has "connected the dots," helping you identify how the trends on the global level are affecting life on the local level.

The additions to this book have added a great deal of information which provides a picture of a very empowered world system—politically (the empowerment of the United Nations), environmentally (sustainable development and Gaia worship), economically (public-private partnerships—fascism), and financially (the empowerment of the World Bank and International Monetary Fund). This empowerment could not be possible without the help and guidance of the United States federal government. Both Republicans and Democrats have had a hand in establishing and protecting this global infrastructure. The question is, "what should you do?"

1. You need to determine if I am correct in what I have written. Do your own research. Ask God to show you both truth and discernment. Determine if you want to be used so that you can stand in the gap. Ask Him to to change any incorrect attitudes so that you can be used.
2. Look around your neighborhood, county, and state to determine what is going on. Start attending meetings—school board, country council, zoning, and state hearing, etc. You have to get involved in order to stand in the gap. The final fight for control is at the local and country levels.

3. There are dozens of cities that are already implementing "Agenda 21" and "Sustainable Cities" programs, determine if there is one near you. Start asking questions of your local officials, find out what they know.

4. Only by your action or inaction will the future be determined. The battle is both philosophical and spiritual.

"The effective fervent prayers of a righteous man avails much."

JOAN M. VEON

Businesswoman/Independent Journalist
P. O. Box 77
Middletown, MD 21769

Up until September 1994 Joan Veon was just a businesswoman. As a result of attending the United Nations Conference on Population and Development in Cairo, Egypt, she received her "wake-up call" as she found there was more going on at the global level than most Americans knew, understood, or were being told.

In her determination to understand the global level and what it really means for Americans, Joan has attended over thirty-six UN and UN-related conferences since Cairo on topics ranging from the social to the economic to the environment. The level of conference has varied from the UN mega conferences in Cairo, Copenhagen, Istanbul, and Rome, to IMF/World Bank meetings, to the (4) Group of Seven (now Eight), (4) Group of Seven Finance Ministers meetings, (4) Group of Eight Foreign Ministers meetings, the International Organization for Security Commissions (IOSCO), the Rio Plus Five (follow-up to the Earth Summit), (2) World Economic Forum in Davos, Switzerland, the Second Summit of the Americas in Chile, (3) Bank for International Settlements, the International Criminal Court in Rome, Al Gore's First Global Conference on Reinventing Government, the Global Disaster Information Network, the fiftieth anniversary of NATO, the Shepherdstown Peace Talks, the World Trade Organization meetings in Seattle, and most recently the preparatory meetings for the "People's Millennium Summit" at the United Nations. She has also covered Mikhail Gorbachev's first State of the World Forum in San Francisco, 1995, the UN 50th Anniversary in San Francisco and New York, and the "by-invitation-only" Money Matters II Conference in Boston.

Joan has been credentialed through "USA Radio" and has appeared as a regular guest on the "Michael Reagan Show," the "Derry Brownfield Show," "Radio Liberty," and numerous others across the U.S. She has asked questions of presidents, prime ministers, key United Nations/IMF/World Bank officials, Bank for International Settlements executives, the Bank of England officials, high officials in the Clinton Administration, multinational CEOs, and others in order to understand the global agenda and how it relates to the local level.

In her capacity as a businesswoman for fifteen years, Joan writes a quarterly economic newsletter which has become more global in its analysis in an effort to identify and name key economic players and trends and how they are affecting our pocketbooks. Her firm, Veon Financial Services, Inc., is a Registered Investment Advisor.

Joan's second company, The Women's International Media Group, Inc., provides the opportunity for her to cover and report on the global conferences and is a 501(c)(3) nonprofit. She writes a bi-monthly newsletter documenting the United Nations activities and plans called "UN Watch!"

Lastly, Joan has authored a number of briefing books documenting her research. Her book *Prince Charles: The Sustainable Prince* is in its fourth printing and discusses her belief that when the U.S. Senate signed the UN Charter is when we officially entered world government and also reverted back under British control. She documents this as well as a number of other global issues such as public-private partnerships between the Prince of Wales and the United Nations and World Bank. She shows the real Prince Charles as being a very powerful man to watch!!!

Joan's second book, *The United Nations: Global Straitjacket* is a 400-page handbook on world government. Joan is currently gathering data for several other books and is a popular speaker at conferences.